New Dialogues and Plays for Little Children, Ages Five to Ten

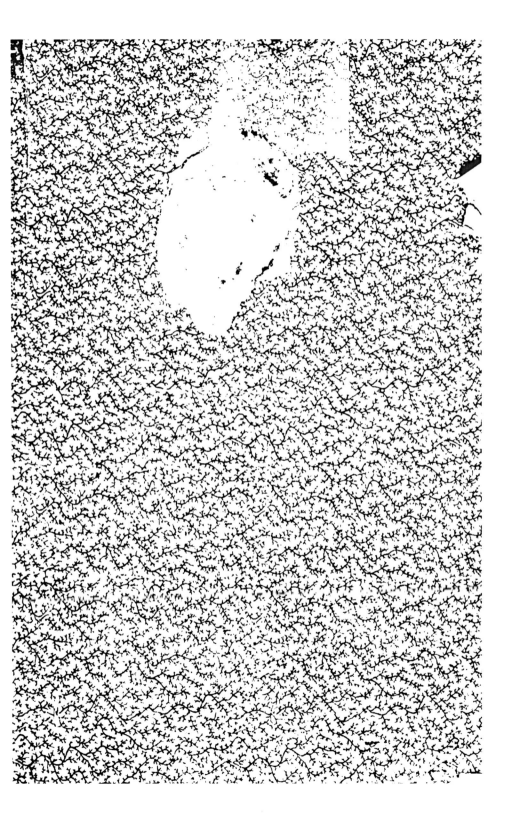

New Dialogues and Plays

FOR LITTLE CHILDREN, AGES FIVE TO TEN

SELECTED FROM THE BOOKLET WORK OF
WELL-KNOWN AUTHORS

HINDS, NOBLE & ELDREDGE, Publishers
31-33-35 WEST FIFTEENTH STREET — NEW YORK

New Dialogues and Plays

FOR LITTLE CHILDREN, AGES FIVE TO TEN

ADAPTED FROM THE POPULAR WORKS OF
WELL-KNOWN AUTHORS

BY

BINNEY GUNNISON

Instructor in the School of Expression, Boston ; formerly Instructor in Elocution in Worcester Academy, and in Brooklyn Polytechnic Institute

HINDS, NOBLE & ELDREDGE, Publishers
31-33-35 WEST 15TH STREET, NEW YORK CITY

PREFACE

It is well known by successful teachers that one of the most efficient means of maintaining interest in all kinds of schools is the well-regulated literary society, and in the literary society the one exercise that "sets the whole community on end" is the play. But a play or dialogue, to be presented on the stage in such a manner as to be helpful as well as entertaining, must be so presented in print that the pupil who is to take part, as well as the teacher who is to manage, may fully understand the external equipment, and in a general way both the theme and the plot of the play.

This is a collection of plays for use in the first grades of the school, and an effort has been made in the introduction to each dialogue to give a bird's-eye view of the stage, the characters, the furniture, the costumes, and the situations in the play.

Those in charge of programs for special occasions in connection with other organizations than those connected with the school work will find many of these plays well adapted to their particular work.

The success of a dialogue depends upon having the right child in the right place, and a teacher or manager who carefully examines these plays will find in them ample suggestion to enable the right placing of the participants each according to his special talents.

We bespeak for this little book a hearty reception by those interested in this line of work.

TABLE OF CONTENTS

HUMOROUS.

SERIOUS.

THE BLUE AND THE GRAY.

CHARACTERS.

Grandmother Lee.

Ruth, Alice, George *and* **Harry,** *her grandchildren.*

Situation.—*On the morning of Memorial Day* GRAND-
MOTHER LEE *is in her sitting-room, seated in an arm-
chair knitting.* GEORGE *is sitting near a table and is
learning a poem which he is to recite at a party in the
evening.*

*The dresses of the grandchildren should all be simple
and conventional.* GRANDMOTHER LEE *should be in
black and wear a white muslin cap; she should have
false powdered curls and wear spectacles.*

RUTH enters listlessly and crosses platform.

RUTH (*looking expectantly to the side*).—I wish Alice and
Harry would come back with those flowers. I'm tired
doing nothing.

GEORGE (*gets up and hands book to Ruth*).—I'll give you
something to do. See if I can repeat " The Blue and the
Gray."

RUTH.—The whole poem ?

GEORGE.—Yes, it's not long, but if you like I'll try only
the second verse. If I know the second I know the others.

RUTH.—Shall I tell you how it begins ?

GEORGE.—Oh, no !   I'll manage.   (*He recites slowly.*)

> From the silence of sorrowful hours
>   The desolate mourners go
> Lovingly laden with flowers,
>   Alike for the friend and the foe :
> Under the sod and the dew
>   Waiting the judgment day,
> Under the roses, the Blue,
>   Under the lilies, the Gray.

(*Grandmother stops knitting and wipes her spectacles.*)

GEORGE.—Didn't I say that well, Grandmother ?

GRANDMOTHER (*very sadly*).—Yes, my boy , but it re-called sad memories.

Enter ALICE *and* HARRY *with roses, lilies and other flowers which they throw on the floor.*

ALICE (*kisses Grandmother*).—Do you think we have gathered enough flowers, Grandmother ?

GRANDMOTHER.—Yes, my dear, I think there will be enough to make one bouquet for each grave.   (*Children sit down on the floor and arrange the flowers.*)

RUTH.—I wonder if the party will be nice to-night.   We met Mrs. Adams and she said she hoped you, Grandmother, would come over with us.

GRANDMOTHER.—I will see.

ALICE.—Did you hear that Mrs. Adams wants a motto to put at each plate ?

HARRY.—Yes, and I have a fine one (*takes paper out of pocket and reads*) "Give Me Liberty or Give Me Death."

GEORGE.—Mine is " Don't Give Up the Ship."

GRANDMOTHER.—And you, girls ?

RUTH.—I like this—" I regret that I have but one life to give to my country."

ALICE.—I heard Grandmother say some time ago that she liked this—" Let Us Have Peace."

GRANDMOTHER.—Yes, Alice, I like your's best.

HARRY (*jumps up and marches around the room*).—I would like to be a soldier, wouldn't you, George ?

GEORGE.—Yes, I want to be a General and command the troops—wear a sword and gold epaulettes.

RUTH.—Do you think war is right, Grandmother ? It seems so cruel.

GRANDMOTHER.—It is cruel, my dear, and some day let us hope we won't have any wars at all.

RUTH.—Grandmother, what makes you look so sad to-day ? Is it because it is Memorial Day ?

GRANDMOTHER.—Yes, my dear, I'm thinking of the first Memorial Day.

GEORGE.—Oh, tell us about it, please.

RUTH (*gets up and leans over Grandmother's chair*).—Did you wish the North or the South to win, Grandmother?

GRANDMOTHER.—I wished neither, Ruth, I only wished that there had been no war.

ALICE (*kneels at Grandmother's feet*).—Were the soldiers of the North right, Grandmother ?

GRANDMOTHER.—Those who fought for both sides thought they were right, my dear, but oh, how I wish the war had never been.

GEORGE.—Will you tell us about your first Memorial Day, Grandmother ?

GRANDMOTHER.—It was not called Memorial Day at first, George. (*She stops knitting and sighs deeply.*) When the war broke out I was much younger than I am now. It's a long time ago. We were then living in New York, although both Grandfather and I belonged to Richmond. My boy, Jack, was at home with us, and Will was with my brother in Richmond. Jack thought the North was right and joined the Blues. Will, who was with his uncle, fought for the Grays. (*Takes off spectacles and wipes them.*)

HARRY.—How old were they ? (*Gets up with some roses and lilies in his hand. Puts flowers on table and sits down.*)

GRANDMOTHER.—Jack was twenty, and Will was only eighteen.

HARRY.—And were they both killed ?

GRANDMOTHER.—Yes. (*They all listen intently.*) My bonny boys both lost their lives at the siege of Richmond, Will in the winter time and Jack in the spring. They are buried side by side. The days of the war were sad, sad days. Many a heart was broken then. Every year since my brave boys first slept in the churchyard I have gathered flowers to place on their graves. Others who had lost their dear ones have done the same.

GEORGE.—Isn't it right to decorate the graves of Northern and Southern soldiers alike ?

GRANDMOTHER.—It has always seemed right to me. My boys were both my boys, whether they fought for the North or the South.

ALICE.—Dear Grandmother. (*Puts her arms around her.*) I shall always decorate Confederate and Union graves alike. We have lilies and roses here, which shall be for the Union soldiers ?

RUTH.—The roses.

HARRY.—And the lilies for the Confederates.

ALICE.—Help me gather them up and put them in water. (*They all begin to pick up the flowers except Grandmother.*)

GEORGE (*arranging the flowers*)—
> Under the sod and the dew,
> Waiting the Judgment Day,
> Under the roses, the Blue,
> Under the lilies, the Gray.

GRANDMOTHER (*picks up a rose and a lily from table and kisses them, then she leans down on the table and sobs.*)

ELSIE'S BURGLAR.

CHARACTERS.

Elsie, *a little girl of seven.*

A Burglar, *a wiry, dark-complexioned man, in soiled clothes, slouch hat, and noiseless shoes.*

Situation.—*Elsie's father, an editor, has been suddenly called away from his home in London and has told the little girl to take good care of her mother in his absence. Burglars have plundered the next house the night before and little* ELSIE *is watchful. She hears a noise, suspects a burglar is the cause of it, and hurries down to prevent any disturbance of her mother. While the household sleeps, the following dialogue takes place in the pantry, or kitchen, or perhaps dining-room.*

The burglar must have some tools, a bunch of keys and a bag. ELSIE *needs only a pretty little box which contains her jewels; and she must appear in her little night-dress. The platform must contain a sideboard with drawers in it for table silver. On the table or sideboard must be a decanter of wine and some glasses. There must be a window arranged for the entrance and exit of the burglar.*

The pantry of a well furnished house. A BURGLAR *enters through the window and shortly after* ELSIE *in her night-dress enters by the door. The* BURGLAR *starts back at sight of her.*

6

ELSIE (*in a soft voice*).—Don't be frightened. I don't want to hurt you. I came to ask a favor of you. (*He stares at her.*) You see I couldn't hurt you if I wanted to. I'm too little. I'm only seven—and a little over—and I'm not going to scream, because that would waken mamma, and that's just what I don't want to do.

BURGLAR (*in a whisper*).—Well, I'll be blowed if this ain't a rummy go! (*He laughs hard but without noise.*) The rummiest go! An' she hain't agoin' to 'urt me. Oh, my heye!

ELSIE (*gently*).—If you please, are you really a burglar?

BURGLAR.—Lor', no, miss, by no manner o' means. I'm a dear friend o' yer par's, come to make a evenin' call, an' not a-wishin' to trouble the servants, I stepped in through the winder.

ELSIE (*gravely*).—Ah! I see you are joking with me, as papa does sometimes. But what I wanted to say to you was this: Papa has gone to Scotland, and all our servants are women, and mamma would be so frightened if you were to waken her, that I am sure it would make her ill. And if you are going to burgle, would you please burgle as quietly as you can, so that you wont disturb her?

BURGLAR.—Well, I'll be blowed!

ELSIE.—Why don't you say "I'll be blown"? I'm sure it isn't correct to say you'll be blowed.

BURGLAR (*muttering to himself*).—There hain't no time to waste.

ELSIE.—Nó, I suppose there isn't. Mamma might wake and miss me. What are you going to burgle first?

BURGLAR (*moodily*).—You'd better go upstairs to yer mar.

ELSIE (*thoughtfully*).—You oughtn't to burgle anything. Of course you know that, but if you have really made up your mind to do it, I would like to show you the things you'd better take.

BURGLAR.—What, fer instance?

ELSIE.—You mustn't take any of mamma's things, because they are all in her room, and you would waken her, and besides, she said it would break her heart; and don't take any of the things papa is fond of. I'll tell you what—you can take my things.

BURGLAR.—What kinds o' things?

ELSIE.—My locket and the little watch papa gave me, and the necklace and bracelets my grandmamma left me, they are worth a great deal of money, and they are very pretty, and I was to wear them when I grew to be a young lady, but—you can take them. And—then—(*with a sigh*) there are—my books. I'm very fond of them, but——

BURGLAR.—I don't want no books just at present for I haven't time to read 'em.

· ELSIE.—Don't you? Ah, thank you.

BURGLAR.—Well, (*staring hard at her*) I never see no sich a start afore.

ELSIE.—Shall I go upstairs and get the other things?

BURGLAR.—No. You stay where you are. (*He opens drawers and takes out silver knives and forks, etc., and busies himself in tying them up.*)

ELSIE (*after watching him a while*).—Is your business a good one?

BURGLAR.—'Tain't as good as it ought to be, by no manner o' means. Every one hain't as hobliging as you, my little dear.

ELSIE.—Oh! You know you obliged me by not making a noise.

BURGLAR.—Well, as a rule, we don't make a practice o' makin' no more noise than we can help. It hain't considered 'ealthy in the perfession.

ELSIE.—Would you mind leaving us a few forks and spoons to eat with, if you please? I beg pardon for interrupting you, but I'm afraid we shall not have any to use at breakfast.

BURGLAR.—Hain't yer got no steel uns?

ELSIE.—Mamma wouldn't like to use steel ones, I'm sure. I'll tell you what you can do. Please leave out enough for mamma, and I can use steel. I don't care about myself much. (*He hesitates, then does as she asks, and even leaves out her little fork and spoon and knife.*) Oh! you are very kind.

BURGLAR.—That's a reward o' merit, cos yer didn't squeal. (*He busies himself with the silver in silence.*)

ELSIE (*after a moment's thought*).—Would you really rather be a burglar than anything else?

BURGLAR.—Well, p'r'aps I'd prefer to be Lord Mayor, or a member o' the 'Ouse o' Lords, or heven the Prince o' Wales, honly for there bein' hobstacles in the way of it.

ELSIE.—Oh! you couldn't be the Prince of Wales, you know. I meant wouldn't you rather be in some other profession? My papa is *an editor*. How would you like to be an editor?

BURGLAR.—Well, hif yer par ud change with me, or hif he chanced to know hany heditor with a roarin' trade as ud be so hobligin' as to 'and it hover, hits wot I've allers 'ad a leanin' to.

ELSIE.—I am sure papa would not like to be a burglar; but perhaps he might speak to his friends about you, if you would give me your name and address, and if I were to tell him how obliging you were, and if I told him you really didn't like being a burglar.

BURGLAR (*putting his hand in his pocket with apparent surprise*).—To think o' me a-forgettin' my card-case an' a leavin' it on the pianner when I come hout! I'm sich a bloomin' forgetful cove. I might hev knowed I'd hev wanted it.

ELSIE.—It is a pity. But if you told me your name and your number, I think I could remember it.

BURGLAR (*regretfully*).—I'm afeard yer couldn't, but I'll try yer. Lord Halgernon Hedward Halbert de Penton-ville, Yde Park. Can you think o' that?

ELSIE.—Are you a lord? Dear me, how strange!

BURGLAR.—It is sing'lar; I've hoften thought so myself. But not wishin' to detain a lady no longer than can be helped, s'pose we take a turn in the lib'ery among yer respected par's things.

ELSIE.—Don't make a noise. (*She leads the way to the side but stops, hesitates and turns back.*) Oh, please, do me another favor, won't you? Please let me slip quietly upstairs and bring down my own things instead. They will be so easy to carry away, and they are very valuable, and—and I will make you a present of them if you will not touch anything that belongs to papa. He is so fond of his things and besides that he is so good.

BURGLAR (*grumblingly*).—Go and get yer gim-cracks. (*She goes out. While she is gone he eats a piece of pie and pours out a glass of wine from the decanter. Just as he is about to drink the wine she enters and he sets down the glass.*)

ELSIE (*handing a little box to him*).—Papa gave me the watch, and mamma gave me the locket; and the pearls were grandmamma's, and grandmamma is in heaven.

BURGLAR (*taking the box of treasures and raising the glass*).—Yer 'e'lth, my dear, an' 'appy returns an' many on 'em. May yer grow up a hornyment to yer sect, an' a comfort to yer respected mar an' par. (*He throws his head far back and drains the glass to the bottom; then he takes up his bundles of silver and prepares to go.*)

ELSIE.—Are you going away?

BURGLAR.—Yes, my dear, I'm going d'rectly.

ELSIE.—Can you wait till I show you a little book that mamma gave me?

BURGLAR.—Why, certainly. I'll wait an hour for you, my little dear. I'm awfully fond of books, I am. (*Elsie retires.*)

BURGLAR (*soliloquizes*). This is a business I don't like. That kid makes me ashamed of myself. I feel as if I couldn't take anything as she'd ever touched.

ELSIE (*returns with book*).—Will you please write your name in this book. It's my birthday book. I got it from mamma on my last birthday.

BURGLAR (*takes book and looks at inscription on it. Reads aloud*). "To Elsie, my dear daughter, on her sixth birthday," and then asks: Is your name Elsie?

ELSIE.—Yes, and that is mamma's name, too.

BURGLAR (*stands staring at the book and soliloquizes*).— Elsie, Elsie, oh, my God, and that was the name of my wife and our little un, dead now twenty years. I was a better man when they were alive and, please God, I'll change my life yet. (*To Elsie.*) My little dear, meeting with you has reminded me of those that are dead long ago, and made me a new man. I'll never steal anything again.

ELSIE.—Oh, I am so glad that you are going to be good.

BURGLAR (*lays down his bundles and says*).—When your par comes home, Elsie (*breaks down when he says Elsie*), tell him a bad man came in here but went away a better man an' stealin' nothin'. You'll find everything in them bundles.

ELSIE.—Papa will be sorry he didn't see you.

BURGLAR.—No, my dear, he won't. Some day I may see him and tell him how good and brave you are. Now, will you shake hands and say " Good-bye, and God bless you ? "

ELSIE.—Good-bye and God bless you.

BURGLAR.—Good-bye, good-bye (*and swiftly disappears*).

ELSIE.—Poor man, he seemed so unhappy. Oh, how I wish his little Elsie had lived, because then he wouldn't be a burglar. I wonder what papa will say when I tell him all about it.

AUNT ELLEN'S HATCHET.

CHARACTERS.

Aunt Ellen, *a young lady, gentle and attractive to children.*

Gladys, *a very small girl.*

Alice, Ida, *two other girls not quite so small.*

Harry, *a small boy.*

Situation.—AUNT ELLEN *is entreated by the children for a story. She tells one which stirs up the consciences of them all so that at the end of the story they confess to several ludicrous sins.*

They all sit in a curve about AUNT ELLEN, *who has an arm-chair in the center of the platform. The best order is* HARRY, GLADYS, AUNT ELLEN, ALICE, IDA. *Let the children show all the interest they feel at the story* AUNT ELLEN *tells. The interest of the audience depends on the interest the children feel and show.*

Enter AUNT ELLEN *and* HARRY, IDA, ALICE *and* GLADYS, *with some confusion.*

ALICE.—You will tell us a story, won't you, auntie?

AUNT ELLEN (*scanning their faces*).—You really want a story, do you?

ALL.—Oh, yes, yes!

AUNT ELLEN.—Well, come sit down and be quiet, then. (*They take seats, with Gladys next to Aunt Ellen.*)

ALICE (*after they are seated*).—A fairy story, you know.

AUNT ELLEN.—A fairy story? I don't know about that. I told a little boy a fairy story once, and he went right off and whispered to his mother that I was a very wicked lady, for the story wasn't true, not a bit.

HARRY.—Poh! he was a smart boy.

AUNT ELLEN.—I don't like to be called a wicked lady, you know.

ALICE.—There now, auntie, don't you s'pose we know they're only play-stories? Just as if we hadn't a speck of sense!

AUNT ELLEN (*covering her eyes with her fingers*).—Well, let me see. Once upon a time, when the moon was full—

GLADYS.—Full of what? (*She looks straight up into Aunt Ellen's face.*) Full of fairies?

AUNT ELLEN (*stroking Gladys's hair*).—When the moon was round, my child. But wait. I'll tell a story Gladys can understand—wouldn't you, my dears? When I was a little girl—

ALL.—That's right. Oh, tell about that. (*They settle themselves to listen.*)

GLADYS.—Was you about as big as me? And was your name *little Ellen?*

AUNT ELLEN.—Yes, they called me little Ellen sometimes, and sometimes Nellie. When I was about as old as Alice, I happened to go into the back-room one day, and saw Uncle William's hatchet lying on the meat-block. I knew I had no right to touch it, but it came into my head that I would try to break open some clams. The hatchet, instead of cracking the shells, came down with full force on my foot! (*The children start.*) I had on thick boots, but it cut through my right boot deep into the bone. Oh, how I screamed!

ALICE (*looking scared*).—I should think you would, auntie. Did it bring the blood?

AUNT ELLEN.—Yes, indeed! Why, when I went into the kitchen, my footsteps were tracked with little pools of blood, oozing out of my boot. Sister Maria screamed out, "Oh, look at Nellie! She's cut her foot with that hatchet." "No, no, I haven't," I said, for I was afraid of being punished. You see, father had forbidden us little ones ever to touch that hatchet.

ALICE (*looking shocked*).—Why, you told a right up and down—fib.

HARRY (*shaking his head*).—A real whopper.

AUNT ELLEN.—So I did, children, and before my story is done, you shall see what misery my sin caused me.

GLADYS.—Did Mr. 'Gustus Allen know about it?

AUNT ELLEN (*looking very self-conscious and blushing*). —I guess not. He lived ever so far off then.

GLADYS.—Oh, dear. I wish he hadn't gone to the wars. How it made you cry!

ALICE.—Hush up, please, can't you, Gladys? Aunt Ellen is telling a story.

AUNT ELLEN.—Well, they sent for the doctor in great haste, and then tried to pull off my boot; but my foot was so badly swollen and bleeding so fast, that it took a great while. I can't tell how long, for I fainted. It was ever so long before I could walk a step. Every time anybody spoke of my hurt, I said, "Why, I was just coming into the house with those clams, and my foot slipped and I fell and hit me on something. I don't know whether it was a hatchet or a stick of wood; but I never touched the hatchet!"

IDA.—There, I shouldn't have thought that of *you*, auntie.

HARRY.—Poh! they must have known you was a-foolin'; of course they did.

AUNT ELLEN.—Well, I knew nobody believed me. The hatchet had been found red with blood, and mother looked,

O, so sad! but I had told that falsehood so many times that it did seem as if I hadn't any courage left to tell the truth. It had grown to be very easy to keep saying, "I never *touched* the hatchet."

ALICE (*whispering to Ida*).—Makes me think of that play. "My father's lost his hatchet."

AUNT ELLEN.—Every one tried to amuse me while I was sick, but there was always a thorn in my pillow.

GLADYS.—A thorn?

AUNT ELLEN.—Not a real thorn, dear. I mean I had told a wrong story, and I couldn't feel happy. (*Here Alice turns away her head and looks far away*). I got well, only I limped a little. Then it was almost time to think of making presents for the Christmas tree. I didn't like to have Christmas come while I was feeling so. I talked it over with myself a great while though, and at last I said, "I *will*; I'll do it." First, I asked God to forgive me and help me. Then I went into the parlor where your grandfather was—he wasn't deaf then. I thought I should choke. I caught hold of one of the buttons on his coat, and spoke as fast as I could. "O father, I've told more than a hundred thousand lies. I *did* take that hatchet! Will you forgive me?

ALICE.—Did he?

AUNT ELLEN.—Forgive! I guess he did! My dear child, it was just what he had been waiting to do. Oh, and the way he talked to me about lying, I shall never, never forget if I live to be a hundred years old.—I believe that's about all the story there is to it, children.

IDA.—Well, I'm much obliged to you, auntie; I think it's just as nice as a fairy story—don't you, Alice?

ALICE (*looking confused*).—I don't know, I'm sure.—See here, auntie, I've lost your gold ring!

AUNT ELLEN.—My ring?   I forgot that I let you take it.

ALICE.—Don't you know I asked you for it when you stood by the table making bread?   And it slipped off my finger this afternoon into the water barrel!

AUNT ELLEN.—Why, Alice!

ALICE.—And I was a coward, and didn't dare to tell you, auntie.   Sometime when you asked for it, I was going to say, "Hadn't you better take a pair of tongs and see if it isn't in the water-barrel?

AUNT ELLEN.—Oh, Alice!

IDA.—She isn't any worse than me, auntie.   Ma asked me how the mud came on my handkerchief, and I said Gladys wiped my boots with it.   And so she did, auntie, but I told her to.   And wasn't I such a coward for laying it off on little Gladys?

AUNT ELLEN.   I am glad you have told me the whole truth now, though it does make me feel sad, too, for it's too much like my hatchet story.   Oh, do remember from this time, children, and never, never *dare* be *cowards* again. (*She rises.*)   Come children, it's time for pleasant dreams now, and kisses all round.   (*They go out.*)

2

THE NEW BABY.

Small Person, *a little girl of seven.*

Annie, *another little girl, her Best Friend.*

A Nurse, *with a tiny baby or large doll.*

Situation.—*Two little girls are walking abroad toward dusk, when they see a woman approaching with a baby in her arms. They are all eagerness to see. Then follows this dialogue.*

Enter SMALL PERSON *and* ANNIE.

SMALL PERSON.—There is a lady with a baby, and it looks like a new one.

ANNIE.—It is a new one. She isn't a Square lady, I wonder who she is.

SMALL PERSON (*almost in a whisper*).—Would she think it rude if we spoke to her?

ANNIE.—Oh, we don't know her. She might think it very rude.

SMALL PERSON.—Do you think she would? She looks kind.

ANNIE.—Let us walk past her.

Enter NURSE, *with baby in her arms; the children pass by, looking up into her face, and she smiles at them.*

ANNIE (*nudging the other*).—Let's ask her. You do it.

18

SMALL PERSON.—No, you.

ANNIE.—I daren't.

SMALL PERSON.—I daren't, either.

ANNIE.—Oh, *do*. It's a perfectly new one.

SMALL PERSON.—Oh, *you* do it. See how nice she looks. (*The Nurse has turned back and they all meet again.*) If you please, isn't that a new baby?

NURSE.—Yes, do you want to look at it?

BOTH.—Oh, yes, please. We do love them so.

NURSE (*she stoops down, turns the white lace veil back and shows the face*).—There.

SMALL PERSON.—Oh, isn't it a *beautiful* one!

ANNIE.—Is it a *very* new one?

NURSE.—Yes, very new.

SMALL PERSON.—*How* new?

NURSE.—Only a month. Are you so very fond of babies?

ANNIE.—We love them better than anything in the world.

NURSE.—Better than dolls?

SMALL PERSON.—Oh, thousands better!

NURSE.—But dolls don't cry.

SMALL PERSON.—If I had a baby, it wouldn't cry, because I should take such care of it.

NURSE.—Would you like a baby of your own?

SMALL PERSON.—I would give worlds and worlds for one!

NURSE.—Would you like me to give you this one?

SMALL PERSON (*breathlessly*).—*Give* it to me? Oh, you couldn't.

NURSE.—I think I could if you would be sure to take care of it.

SMALL PERSON.—Oh, oh! but its mamma wouldn't let you.

NURSE (*reflectively*).—Yes, I think she would. You see, she has enough of them.

SMALL PERSON (*gasping with incredulity*). — Ah! you —you're making fun of me.

NURSE.—No, I am not at all. They are very tiresome when there are a great many of them. What would you do with this one if I gave it to you?

SMALL PERSON (*eagerly*).—I would wash it every morning. I would wash it in a little bath, and with a big soft sponge and Windsor soap—and I would puff it all over with powder —and dress it and undress it—and put it to sleep, and walk it about the room—and trot it on my knees—and give it milk.

NURSE (*seriously*).—It takes a great deal of milk.

SMALL PERSON.—I would ask Mamma to let me take it from the milkman. I'm sure she would, I would give it as much as it wanted, and it would sleep with me, and I would buy it a rattle, and—

NURSE.—I see you know how to take care of it. You shall have it.

SMALL PERSON (*fearfully*).—But how can its mamma *spare* it? Are you sure she could spare it?

NURSE.—Oh, yes, she can spare it. Of course I must take it back to her to-night and tell her you want it, and I have promised it to you; but to-morrow evening you can have it.

SMALL PERSON.—Oh, really, can I?

NURSE.—Yes. Goodby. (*She goes out.*)

SMALL PERSON.—Goodby. Oh, Annie, won't we have a nice time with a new baby? Come home and tell Mamma all about it. (*They go out.*)

THE UNBURIED WOMAN.

Mr. Bright, *a cheerful old gentleman.*

Mrs. Pokabout, Mrs. Talket, Mrs. Goround, *three old ladies, full of curiosity, and dressed in old-fashioned costumes.*

Situation.—MRS. POKABOUT *and* MRS. TALKET *are hunting for news when they meet* MR. BRIGHT. *He tells them about a woman who is denied burial, and then he hurries away. After a while he returns to clear up the mystery and laugh at the gossipers.*

Little folks should dress up and play these old folks. The old women are looking about all the time to find something wrong. The scene is on a street-corner and so very little is needed to decorate the platform.

MRS. POKABOUT *and* MRS. TALKET *enter from one side.* MR. BRIGHT *enters from the other side. They meet.*

MRS. POKABOUT.—Have you heard any news, Mrs Talket?

MRS. TALKET.—News? no, I am dying to hear some. I haven't heard a word since last night, and here it is noon.

MR. BRIGHT.—I heard something as I came along, and you wouldn't believe it, though I received it from a person who tells the truth and knew the fact, and so he couldn't make a mistake.

MRS. TALKET.—Oh, tell it to us. I hope it is somebody run away.

MRS. POKABOUT.—I hope it is a murder or a suicide. We haven't had any good news these two months.

MR. BRIGHT.—It is neither one. There is a woman down in the village and they will not let her be buried.

MRS. TALKET.—You don't say so!

MR. BRIGHT.—I do. They positively refuse to bury her.

MRS. POKABOUT.—Do tell! What could the poor creature have done to be denied burial?

MR. BRIGHT.—I do not know what the trouble was, but they say the coroner has his reasons, and buried she shall not be.

MRS. POKABOUT.—Where is she lying? I must go and inquire into it. Bless me, Mrs. Talket, how could this happen and we not hear of it?

MRS. TALKET.—Did you hear her name, Mr. Bright? that may give us a clue.

MR. BRIGHT.—I did not learn her name, though, if I forget not, it began with a G, —— or some such letter. But I have a little errand up the street, and must leave you. In the meantime, as we know so little, it will be wise not to repeat what I have told you. Good morning. (*He goes out.*)

MRS. POKABOUT.—Did you ever hear of anything so strange? One of two things is certain, she has either killed herself or been killed, and is kept for examination.

MRS. TALKET.—I don't understand it so. Mr. Bright seemed to say that she had been lying a long time, and was not to be buried at all. But here comes Mrs. Goround, and perhaps she can tell us all about it, as she comes fresh from the village.

MRS. GOROUND *enters.*

MRS. POKABOUT.—Good-morning, Mrs. Goround.

MRS. GOROUND.—Good-morning, Mrs. Pokabout. How do you do, Mrs. Talket?

MRS. TALKET.—Pretty well, I thank you. How do you do?

MRS. GOROUND.—Not very well, I'm much obliged to you. I've had a touch of hydrophoby, I believe they call it, or something else.

MRS. POKABOUT. (*to Mrs. Talket*).—Nothing new. She always hated cold water. (*Aloud.*) How did the dreadful disease affect you, Mrs. Goround ! What dog bit you?

MRS. GOROUND.—Dog ! What do you mean by a dog? The disease began with a cold in my head, and a sore throat and—

MRS. TALKET.—Oh, it was the influenza.

MRS. GOROUND.—So it was. I knew it was some outlandish name, and they all sound alike to me. I wish there *was* no foreign words.

MRS. POKABOUT.—Mrs. Goround, did you hear the dreadful news in the village?

MRS. GOROUND.—No. What dreadful news? I have not heard *nothing*, good or bad.

MRS. POKABOUT.—What ! haven't you heard of the woman in the village that they won't bury?

MRS. GOROUND.—Not a word. Who is she? What's her name?

MRS. TALKET.—Her name begins with G., and as that begins your name, I hoped you would know something about it.

MRS. GOROUND.—Bless me ! I never heard a syllable of it ! Why don't they bury the poor thing? I couldn't refuse to bury even a dog.

MRS. POKABOUT.—There is a suspicion of murder or suicide in the case.

MRS. GOROUND.—Well, they hang murderers and suicides, don't they? What can be the matter? There is something very strange about it.

MRS. TALKET.—I am dying to know all about it. Come, let's all go down to the village, and find out. I love to get hold of a mystery.

MRS. POKABOUT.—I say, let us all go, and here is Mr. Bright coming back. He will go with us, for he told us the news and he is dying to learn the particulars.

MR. BRIGHT *comes in again.*

MR. BRIGHT.—Good morning again, ladies.

ALL.—Good morning.

MRS. GOROUND.—What was the matter with that-*air* woman that they won't bury in the village.

MR. BRIGHT.—Nothing is the matter with her.

MRS. GOROUND.—Then in *marcy's* name, why don't they bury her?

MR. BRIGHT.—I know only one reason, but that is a very good one.

MRS. POKABOUT.—We did not know you knew the reason they wouldn't bury her. Why didn't you tell us what it was?

MR. BRIGHT.—You did not ask me, and besides it is somewhat of a secret.

MRS. TALKET.—You need not fear our speaking of it. Hurry and tell us.

MRS. POKABOUT.—Yes, yes. I am bursting with curiosity.

MRS. GOROUND.—And I too, Mr. Bright; you say there is but one reason why they do not bury the woman, and now what is that? (*He looks about with a smile.*)

MRS. POKABOUT.—What is it?

MRS. TALKET.—Yes, what is it?

ALL (*earnestly*).—What is it?

MR. BRIGHT. (*going out*).—She is not dead!

ALL (*rushing after him*).—You horrid——(*They go out.*)

PLAYING "HOOKEY."

Horace, *a small boy, with two fishing poles.*

Prudy, *a smaller girl, with a tin dipper.*

A Voice within.

Situation.—Prudy *has gone out to pick currants. She suddenly sees her cousin* Horace, *who has come from the West to spend a year. He is on the other side of the bushes and he persuades her to go down to the river to fish. Afterward his conscience troubles him for playing truant;* Prudy *gets no bites. Just then her aunt's voice calls and they hurry away home.*

A row of currant bushes extend down one side of the platform with only one small opening. Various devices may be used to secure this effect, a row of plants, a set of real currant bushes, even a fence. The river is supposed to run along in front of the platform which forms the bank of the stream. There should be some means of propping up Prudy's *pole for her, and some rock for her to sit on.*

Enter Prudy, *with a tin dipper to pick currants in, and* Horace *with fishing-rods, on opposite sides of the platform and of the row of currant bushes.*

Prudy.—I thought you was to school!

HORACE (*pulling his hat over his eyes with shame*).— Well, I ain't. The teacher don't keep no order, and I won't go to such a school, so there !

PRUDY.—They don't want *me* to go, 'cause I should know too much. I can say all my letters now, right down straight, 'thout looking on, either.

HORACE.—Oh, ho ! you can't say 'em skipping about, and I shouldn't care if I was you. But you ought to know how to fish, Miss. Don't you wish you could drop in your line, and catch 'em the way I do?

PRUDY (*dropping her dipper and looking through plants*). —Do they like to have you catch 'em ; don't it hurt?

HORACE.—Hurt? Not as I know of. They needn't bite if they don't want to.

PRUDY (*looking wise*).—No, I s'pose they want to get out, and that's why they bite. Of course, when fishes stay in the water much it makes 'em drown.

HORACE (*laughing*).—Oh, my stars ! you ought to live "out west," you're such a cunning little spud. Come, now, here's another fish-pole for you. I'll show you how to catch one, and I'll bet 't will be a polywog—you're just big enough.

PRUDY.—But grandma didn't say I might go down to the river. Wait till I go ask her. (*She starts back.*)

HORACE.—Poh ! no, you needn't ; I have to hurry. Grandma *always* likes it when you go with me, Prudy, because you see I'm a boy, and she knows I can take care of you twice as well as Grace and Susy can.

PRUDY (*clapping her hands*).—Oh, they won't any of 'em know I can fish, and how they'll laugh. How'll I get over there?

HORACE.—Give us your bonnet, and then you "scooch" down, and I'll pull you through. (*She lies down flat on the floor and stretches out her hands. He grabs them and pulls her through between two bushes.*) There, now, I've been and put a bait on the end of your hook, and I plump it in the water—so (*he throws the line over the edge of the platform*). You just hold on to the pole.

PRUDY.—But it jiggles—it tips me. (*She falls down.*)

HORACE.—Well, that's smart ! (*He picks her up.*) There you sit down next time, and I'll prop up the pole with a rock—this way. (*He props up the pole with two rocks.*) There, now, you hold it a little easy, and when you feel a nibble you let me know.

PRUDY (*shaking the line*).—What's a nibble?

HORACE.—A nibble? Why, it's a bite. (*They sit very quiet for some time.*)

PRUDY.—Now, now ! I've got a nibble ! (*Horace springs up to catch her line*). I feel it right here on my neck; I s'pose it's a fly.

HORACE. (*going back to his own line*).—Now look here, you're a little too bad. You made me drop my line just when I was going to have a nibble. Wait till you feel the string wiggle, and then speak, but don't scream. (*They sit still a while longer.*)

PRUDY (*with a groan*).—Oh, dear ! I never did see such fishes. I guess they don't want to be catched.

HORACE.—There, now you've spoke again, and scared one away. If it hadn't been for you I should have got I don't know how many by this time. (*Prudy begins to cry.*) Poh ! crying about that? You're a nice little girl if you do talk too much, so don't you cry. (*Prudy dries her eyes and looks cheerful again.*) I'll tell you what it is, I don't think I make much playing " hookey."

PRUDY.—I don't like playing " hookey," neither, 'cause the hooks won't catch 'em.

HORACE (*laughing*).—Oh, you don't know what I mean. When we boys " out west " stay out of school, we call *that* playing " hookey."

PRUDY.—Oh, do you? But I want to go home now, if we can't catch any nibbles.

A VOICE WITHIN.—Prudy! Prudy!

HORACE.—There, now, there's Aunt Madge calling you. You give me your fish-pole. Can you crawl through the bushes?

PRUDY.—I don't know. I guess you'll have to push some. (*She scratches through while Horace pushes.*)

HORACE.—Now hurry up but don't you tell her that I was here. I'll go round the other way. (*Prudy goes out on one side and Horace on the other.*)

WILLIE (*after a long silence*).—Are they real flowers, mamma, or only make believe?

MRS. HARMON.—They are artificial, Willie. Be a good boy, now, and don't talk any more.

WILLIE.—Yes'm. (*A very long pause*). Mamma!

MRS. HARMON.—'Sh, Willie! What is it?

WILLIE.—When Johnnie-jump-ups are growed up, do they get to be jumpin-jacks?

MRS. HARMON (*with a struggle to keep from smiling*).— Oh, no, dear.

WILLIE.—Why not?

MRS. HARMON.—There, dear. Listen to the sermon.

WILLIE.—What do they get to be?

MRS. HARMON (*with a look of despair*).—They don't get to be anything. They stay just what they are.

WILLIE (*after another silence*).—Mamma, the preacher said "thudly." How many morelys will he——

MRS. HARMON.—'Sh, Willie!

WILLIE.—Yes'm, but I'm getting awfully tired.

MRS. HARMON.—It will only last a little while longer, dear. Be quiet.

WILLIE.—Yes'm. (*A pause.*) Mamma, can a woman be real, real good if she wears a stuffed humming-bird on her bonnet?

MRS. HARMON.—Willie, if you don't hush I shall have to punish you.

WILLIE.—Right here?

MRS. HARMON.—No; after we get home. 'Sh!

WILLIE (*after a thoughtful pause*).—Mamma, seems to me that I've been 'sh-ing a mighty long time! How much longer is he going to——

MRS. HARMON (*with determination*).—Willie, if you say another word I'll take you right out of church.

WILLIE (*his face lights up*).—I won't say another word, mamma, but I'm getting jus horrid tired, and I don't see how I can set still another minute, and I wish he'd quit talkin'—ain't you tired 'most to death—how much longer is he going to keep on—what's the use of bringing me here, anyhow—(*His mother takes him down from his seat and marches him out of church. He looks back with a triumphant smile*).

THE INKSTAND.

CHARACTERS.

Dollie, *a very little girl.*

Amy, Minnie, *two larger girls with aprons on.*

Robbie, *a small boy.*

Aunt Anna, *an irritable woman of middle age.*

Aunt Martha, *a woman of same age with muslin cap on and a white apron.*

Bridget, *a servant of Aunt Martha, with sleeves rolled up and apron on.*

Situation.—AUNT ANNA *has brought over the girls to spend the day with their* AUNT MARTHA. ROBBIE *has been deputed to show them over the house and has at last reached* BRIDGET'S *room.* DOLLIE *finds an inkstand which* ROBBIE *auctions off to the highest bidder. The ink is spilled on* MINNIE'S *apron and* DOLLIE *is sent after milk to take the stain off. She unwittingly reports the whole disaster and the children are summarily taken home.*

The first scene is in BRIDGET'S *chamber, which contains a washstand, bureau, chairs and table. The second scene is in the kitchen or dining-room where dinner is preparing. There is a table partially set for dinner, with cloth and dishes on it. The inkstand may be empty or filled with water.*

Scene I.

ROBBIE *enters, followed by* AMY, MINNIE *and* DOLLIE.

ROBBIE.—This is Bridget's room.

37

AMY.—Well, I'm dreadful tired.

MINNIE.—So am I. I'm going to sit down a minute. (*All sit but Dollie who goes to the bureau and opens a drawer.*)

AMY.—Look here, Dolly Dinsmore, you mustn't open that drawer.

DOLLIE (*putting in both hands*).—Who owns it?

AMY.—Why, Bridget does, of course.

DOLLIE.—No, she doesn't. God owns this drawer, and he's willing I should look into it as long as I'm a mind to.

AMY.—Well, I'll tell Aunt Anna, you see if I don't. That's the way little paddy girls act that steal things.

DOLLIE.—I ain't a stealer. Now, Amy Rexford, I saw you once, and you was a nippin' cream out of the cream-pot. *You're* a paddy!—Oh, here's a *inkstand!*

MINNIE.—Put it right back, and come away.

ROBBIE (*seizing it from her hand*).—Let me take it. I'm going to put it up at auction. I'm Mr. Nelson, riding horseback. (*He jumps up on a stand.*) I'm ringin' a bell. "O yes! O yes! O yes! Auction at two o'clock! Who'll buy my fine fresh ink?"

AMY.—Please give it to me, it isn't yours.

ROBBIE.—Fresh ink, red as a lobster!

AMY.—This minute!

ROBBIE.—As green as a pea! Who'll bid? Going! Going!

MINNIE (*climbing into a chair and reaching after it*). —Now, do give it to me, Robbie. You ain't fair a bit.

ROBBIE.—Do you say you bid a *bit?* That's ninepence, ma'am. It's yours; going, gone for a ninepence, knocked off to Miss Dinsmore. (*As Robbie hands it to Minnie, she grabs at it and spills the ink over her apron.*)

MINNIE.—Oh, dear, how dreadful!

ROBBIE (*he has climbed down hastily*).—Don't tell that

I did it, you know I didn't mean any harm. Won't you promise me not to tell?

MINNIE.—Yes, I will—O dear, O dear! What is to be done?

AMY.—Come here quick. (*She pulls her to the wash-stand. Dollie thinks Amy is going to put Minnie into the wash bowl and tries to lift her up*).

MINNIE (*catching at a piece of soap*).—I guess this honey soap will take it out. (*They scrub hard at the apron.*)

AMY.—Stop a minute! Soap makes it worse—ma puts on milk.

MINNIE.—O dear! I wish we had some. How can we get it?

AMY.—I'll tell you what we'll do; we'll send Dollie down-stairs to Bridget, to ask for some milk to drink.

DOLLIE.—I like milk and water the best—with sugar in.

AMY.—Well, get that, its just as good; and come right back with it, and don't tell about the ink. (*Dollie goes out.*)

CURTAIN.

Scene II.

The kitchen or dining-room.

AUNT MARTHA *and* BRIDGET *are getting dinner ready.* DOLLIE *enters.*

DOLLIE.—Oh, Bridget, may I have some white tea?

BRIDGET.—White *tay!* and what may that be now?

DOLLIE.—Oh, some white tea in a cup, you know, with sugar. They let me have it every little once in a while.

AUNT MARTHA.—Milk and water, I suppose. Can't you wait till dinner, my dear?

DOLLIE.—But the girls *can't* wait ; they want it now.

AUNT MARTHA.—Oh, it's for the girls, is it?

DOLLIE.—Yes, but when they've washed the apron I can drink the rest—with white sugar in.

AUNT MARTHA.—The apron! What apron?

AUNT ANNA *enters at rear.*

DOLLIE.—Oh, nothing but Minnie's, I told grandma I'd be good, and I did be good; it was n't *me* spilled the ink.

AUNT MARTHA (*stopping her work*).—Ink spilled?

DOLLIE (*beginning to tremble*).—Oh, I ain't goin' to tell! I didn't, did I? They won't *'low* me to tell.

AUNT ANNA (*stepping to the door*).—Children, come down here this instant. What have you been doing?

Enter AMY *and* MINNIE *with crestfallen faces.*

Oh, Minnie Dinsmore, you naughty, naughty child, what have you been into? Who spilled that ink?

MINNIE (*frightened*).—It got tipped over.

AUNT ANNA.—Of course, it got tipped over—but not without hands, you careless girl! Do you get your shaker, and march home as quick as ever you can! I must go with you, I suppose.

AMY.—Oh, Auntie, she wasn't to blame. It——

AUNT ANNA (*briskly*).—Don't say a word. If she was my little girl I'd have her sent to bed. That dress and apron ought to be soaking this very minute. (*She marches the children all off, followed by Aunt Martha.*)

BRIDGET.—It's not much like the child's mother she is. A mother can pass it by when the childers does such capers, and wait till they git more sinse. (*She goes out the other side.*)

THE SWORD.

CHARACTERS.

Lord Carlton, *a kind and polite gentleman.*

Augustus, *his son, haughty and overbearing.*

Henrietta, *his daughter, gentle and shrewd.*

Frank Raynton, William Raynton, Edward Dudley, Charles Dudley, *manly and independent boys, friends to Augustus.*

James, *a servant to Lord Carlton.*

Situation.—Augustus *has a birthday. His father presents him with a sword, which his sister takes to put a ribbon on it. Before she returns it,* Lord Carlton, *fearing that the weapon may prove dangerous in the hands of his impertinent son, substitutes a turkey's feather for the blade. The confusion of the boy is complete. The sword is given to another.*

Both scenes of this dialogue take place in the play-room of Augustus. *Considerable ingenuity may be shown in fitting this room as a parent of taste and wealth would be likely to furnish it. There should be a table on which* Henrietta *may place the dish of cakes.*

Scene I.

The apartment of AUGUSTUS. *Enter* AUGUSTUS, *with a haughty strut.*

AUGUSTUS.—Aha! this is my birthday! They did well to tell me for I should never have thought of it. I shall have some new present from papa. Let's see, what will he give me? James had something under his coat when he went into papa's room. He would not let me go in with him. Ah! If I did not have to act grown up, I'd have made him show me what he was carrying.—But now I shall know. Here comes papa.

LORD CARLTON *comes in, holding in his hand a sword and belt.*

LORD CARLTON.—Ah! there you are, Augustus! I have already wished you joy on your birthday; but that is not enough, is it?

AUGUSTUS.—Oh! papa—but what is that in your hand, there?

LORD CARLTON.—Something that I fear will not become you well. A sword—look! (*He holds it out.*)

AUGUSTUS.—What! is it for me? Oh! give it to me, dear papa; I will be so good and study all the time.

LORD CARLTON.—Ah! if I only thought that! But do you know a sword calls for a man? Whoever wears a sword, must be no longer a child, but should be respectful and well-behaved. It is not the sword that adorns the man, but the man who adorns the sword.

AUGUSTUS.—Oh! never fear me. I shall adorn mine, I promise; and I won't speak to those mean persons——

LORD CARLTON.—Whom do you call those mean persons?

AUGUSTUS.—I mean those who cannot wear a sword—those who are not nobles, as you and I are.

LORD CARLTON.—For my part, I know no mean persons but those who have a wrong way of thinking, and a worse way of behaving; who are disobedient to their parents—rude and unmannerly to others; so that I see many mean persons among the nobility, and many noble among those whom you call mean.

AUGUSTUS.—Yes, that's what I think.

LORD CARLTON.—What were you saying, then, just now, of wearing a sword? It is necessary that ranks should be distinguished in the world. But the most elevated rank only adds more disgrace to the man unworthy to fill it.

AUGUSTUS.—But, papa, it will be no disgrace to me to have a sword, and to wear it.

LORD CARLTON.—No. I mean for you to render yourself worthy of this distinction by your good behavior. Here is your sword, but remember. (*He hands him the sword.*)

AUGUSTUS.—Oh! yes, papa. You shall see! (*He endeavors to put the sword by his side, but cannot. Lord Carlton helps him to buckle it on.*)

LORD CARLTON.—Eh! why, it does not look bad.

AUGUSTUS.—Oh! I knew.

LORD CARLTON.—It becomes you surprisingly. But above all things, remember what I told you. Good-bye! (*Going, he returns.*) I had forgot; I have just sent for a little party of your friends, to spend the day with you. Behave yourself suitably. (*He goes out.*)

AUGUSTUS.—Yes, papa. (*He struts up and down the room, and now and then looks back to see if his sword is behind him.*) This is fine! This is like a gentleman! Let any of your citizens come in my way now. No more familiarity, if they do not wear a sword; and if they don't like it, out with my rapier. But let us see if it has a good blade. (*Drawing his sword and using furious gestures.*) What!

does that man mean to affront me? One—two! Ah! you defend yourself, do you? Die, scoundrel!

Enter HENRIETTA.

HENRIETTA (*who screams on hearing the last words*).— Bless me! Augustus, are you mad?

AUGUSTUS.—Is it you, sister?

HENRIETTA.—Yes, don't you see? But what are you doing with that thing? (*Pointing to the sword.*)

AUGUSTUS.—Doing with it? what a gentleman should do.

HENRIETTA.—And whom are you going to send out of the world?

AUGUSTUS.—Whoever dares insult me.

HENRIETTA.—And if I should happen to be the person——

AUGUSTUS.—You! I warn you. I wear a sword now, you see. Papa made me a present of it.

HENRIETTA.—I suppose to go and kill people, right or wrong.

AUGUSTUS.—Am not I the honorable? If they do not give me the respect due, smack, a box on the ear. And if your little commoner will be impertinent—sword in hand —(*Going to draw it.*)

HENRIETTA.—Oh! leave it in quiet, brother. What is the respect that you demand?

AUGUSTUS.—You shall soon see. My father has just sent for some young fellows. If those little puppies do not behave themselves respectfully, you shall see how I will manage.

HENRIETTA.—Very well; but what must we do, to behave ourselves respectfully toward you?

AUGUSTUS.—In the first place, I insist upon a low bow— very low.

HENRIETTA (*with great seriousness making him a low*

courtesy).—Your lordship's most humble servant. Was that well?

AUGUSTUS.—No joking, Henrietta, or else——

HENRIETTA.—Nay, I am quite serious, I assure you. We ought to inform your little friends, too.

AUGUSTUS.—Oh ! I will have some sport with those fellows ; give one a pull, another a pinch, and play all sorts of tricks on them.

HENRIETTA.—But if those fellows should not like the sport, and return it on the gentleman's ears——

AUGUSTUS.—What ! low, vulgar blood? No ; they have neither hearts nor swords.

HENRIETTA (*with sarcasm*).—Really, papa saw plainly what a hero was concealed in the person of his son, but do you know too, that there is one principal ornament to your sword wanting?

AUGUSTUS.—What is that? (*Unbuckles the belt and looks all over the sword.*) I do not see that there is the least thing wanting.

HENRIETTA.—Really, you are a very clever swordsman. But a sword-knot now ! Ah ! how a blue and silver knot would dangle from that belt !

AUGUSTUS.—You are right, Henrietta. Quick, a handsome knot ! when my little party comes, they shall see me in all my grandeur.

HENRIETTA.—Give it to me, then.

AUGUSTUS (*giving her the sword*).—There, make haste ! You will leave it in my room, on the table, so I may find it when I want it.

HENRIETTA.—Depend on me.

Enter JAMES.

JAMES.—The two Master Dudleys and the Master Rayntons are below.

AUGUSTUS.—Well! cannot they come up?

JAMES.—My lady ordered me to tell you to come and meet them.

AUGUSTUS.—No, no—it is better to wait for them here.

HENRIETTA.—If mamma wants you to go down——

AUGUSTUS.—Well, I shall go right away. Come, what are you doing? Go, hurry, and let me find it on my table. Do you hear? (*Augustus and James go out.*)

HENRIETTA.—The little insolent! Luckily, I have the sword. My papa does not know you so well as I do. But I'll tell him—ah! here he is.

Enter LORD CARLTON.

HENRIETTA.—You are come just in time, papa. I was going to you.

LORD CARLTON.—What is there, then, of so much consequence, to tell me?—But what are you doing with your brother's sword?

HENRIETTA.—I have promised to put a handsome knot on it; but it was only to get it out of his hands. Do not give it to him again, whatever you do.

LORD CARLTON.—Why should I take back a present I have given him?

HENRIETTA.—At least keep it until he becomes more peaceable. I just now found him all alone, laying about him like Don Quixote, and threatening to make his first trial of fencing on his companions that come to see him.

LORD CARLTON.—The little quarreler! If he will use it for his first exploits, they shall not turn out to his honor, I promise you. Give me the sword.

HENRIETTA (*giving him the sword*).—There, sir, I hear him on the stairs.

LORD CARLTON.—Run, make his knot, and bring it to me when it is ready. (*They go out.*)

Scene II.

Enter AUGUSTUS, *with his hat on. Then follow with un-*
covered heads, EDWARD *and* CHARLES DUDLEY, FRANK
and WILLIAM RAYNTON.

EDWARD (*aside to Frank*).—This is a very polite reception !

FRANK (*aside to Edward*).—I suppose it is the fashion
now to receive company with your hat on, and to walk before them into your own house.

AUGUSTUS.—What are you mumbling there?

EDWARD.—Nothing, Mr. Carlton; nothing.

AUGUSTUS.—It is something that I should not hear?

FRANK.—Perhaps.

AUGUSTUS.—Now I insist upon knowing it.

FRANK.—When you have a right to demand it.

EDWARD.—Softly, Raynton—we are in a strange house——

FRANK.—It is still less becoming to be impolite in one's
own house.

AUGUSTUS (*haughtily*).—Impolite ! Impolite ! Is it because I walked before you?

FRANK.—That is the very reason. Whenever we receive
your visits, or those of any other person, we never go in
first.

AUGUSTUS.—You only do your duty. But from you to
me— (*He waves his hand disdainfully*).

FRANK.—What, then, from you to me?

AUGUSTUS.—Are you noble?

FRANK (*to the two Dudleys and his brother*).—Let us
leave him to himself, with his nobility, if you will take my
advice.

EDWARD.—Oh! Mr. Carlton! if you think it beneath

your dignity to keep company with us, why did you invite us here? We did not ask to come.

AUGUSTUS.—I did not invite you; it was my papa.

FRANK.—Then we will go to my lord, and thank him for his civility. At the same time, we shall let him know that his son thinks it a dishonor to receive us. Come, brother.

AUGUSTUS (*stopping him*).—You cannot take a joke, Master Raynton. Why, I am very happy to see you. Papa invited you to please me, for this is my birthday. Please, stay with me.

FRANK.—This is another thing. But be more polite hereafter. I have not a title as you have, but I will not allow any one to insult me, just the same.

EDWARD.—Be quiet, Raynton, we should be good friends.

CHARLES.—This is your birthday, then, Mr. Carlton?

EDWARD.—I wish you many happy returns of it.

FRANK.—So do I, sir; and all manner of prosperity, (*aside*) and particularly that you may grow a little more polite.

WILLIAM.—I suppose you had han some presents.

AUGUSTUS.—Oh! of course.

CHARLES.—Lots of cakes and sweetmeats.

AUGUSTUS.—Ha! ha! cakes! that would be pretty, indeed. I have them every day.

WILLIAM.—Ah! then, it is money. Two or three dollars?

AUGUSTUS (*disdainfully*).—Something better, and which I alone of all here—yes, I alone, have a right to wear. (*Frank and Edward talk aside.*)

WILLIAM. If I had what has been given to you, I could wear it as well as another, perhaps.

AUGUSTUS (*looking at him contemptuously*). — Poor creature! (*To the two elder brothers.*) What, are you both whispering there again.

Enter HENRIETTA, *with a plate of small cakes.*

HENRIETTA.—Young gentlemen.—I hope you are all happy.

FRANK.—We hope you are the same, miss.

EDWARD.—Miss, we would like to have you stay with us.

HENRIETTA.—Sir, you are very obliging. (*To Augustus.*) Mamma has sent you this, to entertain your friends, until the chocolate is ready. James will bring that up presently, and I shall have the pleasure of helping you.

FRANK.—Miss, thank you very much.

AUGUSTUS.—We do not want you here! But now I think of it, my sword-knot!

HENRIETTA.—You will find the sword and the knot in your room. Good-bye, gentlemen, until I see you again.

FRANK.—Shall we see you soon, miss?

HENRIETTA.—I am going to ask mamma. (*She goes out.*)

AUGUSTUS (*sitting down*).—Come, take chairs and sit down. (*They look at each other, and sit down without speaking. Augustus helps the two younger, and then himself, so plentifully that nothing remains for the two elder.*) Stop a moment! They will bring in more, and then I'll give you some.

FRANK.—Oh! no, we do not want it.

AUGUSTUS.—Oh! with all my heart.

EDWARD.—If this be the politeness of——

AUGUSTUS.—I told you before that they will bring us up something else. (*Haughtily.*) You may take it when it comes, or not take it; you understand that?

FRANK (*indignantly*).—Yes, that is plain enough; and we see plainly, too, what company we are in.

EDWARD.—Are you going to begin your quarrels again? Mr. Carlton. Raynton! (*Augustus rises, all the rest also.*)

4

AUGUSTUS (*going up to Frank*).—What company are you in, then?

FRANK (*firmly*).—With a young nobleman, who is very rude and very impudent—who values himself more than he ought—and who does not know how well-bred people should behave.

EDWARD.—We are all of the same opinion.

AUGUSTUS.—I, rude and impudent? Me, a gentleman!

FRANK.—Yes, I say it again—very rude and very impudent—though you were a duke, though you were a prince.

AUGUSTUS (*striking him*).—I'll teach you whom you are talking to. (*Frank goes to lay hold on him. Augustus slips back, goes out, and shuts the door.*)

EDWARD.—Bless me, Raynton, what have you done? He will go to his father, and tell him a thousand stories. What will happen to us?

FRANK.—His father is a good man. I will go to him myself if Augustus does not. He certainly has not invited us here to be insulted by his son.

CHARLES.—He will send us home and complain of us.

WILLIAM.—No; my brother behaved himself properly My papa will know.

FRANK.—Come with me. Let us all go and find Lord Carlton.

AUGUSTUS *enters with his sword undrawn. The two younger boys run, one in a corner and the other behind an arm-chair.* FRANK *and* EDWARD *stand firm.*

AUGUSTUS (*going up to Frank*).—Now, I'll teach you, you little insolent. (*Draws, and instead of a blade, finds a long turkey's feather. He stops short in confusion. The little ones burst into a loud laugh and come up.*)

FRANK.—Come on! let us see your sword!

EDWARD.—Do not make it worse. It is bad enough now.

WILLIAM.—Aha! This was what you alone had a right to wear.

CHARLES (*in mockery*).—What a terrible weapon!

FRANK.—I could punish you, but I blush to take revenge.

EDWARD.—Let us all leave him.

WILLIAM.—Good-bye to you, Mr. Knight of the turkey's feather.

CHARLES (*with mock terror*).—We shall not come again, you are too terrible now. (*As they are going, Frank stops them.*)

FRANK.—Let us stay and see his father. Appearances will be against us.

EDWARD.—You are right. What would he think of us, if we left without seeing him?

LORD CARLTON *comes in. They all put on an air of respect.* AUGUSTUS *goes aside and cries for spite.*

LORD CARLTON (*looking at Augustus with indignation*).—Well, sir, you have honored your sword nobly—shame! sir, shame! (*Augustus sobs, but cannot speak.*)

FRANK.—My lord, pardon this disturbance. From the first moment of our coming, Mr. Carlton received us so——

LORD CARLTON.—Do not be uneasy, my dear little friend. I know all. I was in the next room, and heard, from the beginning, my son's unbecoming speech. He had just been making me the fairest promises. I have suspected his impertinence for a long time, but I wished to see for myself, and for fear of mischief, I put a blade to his sword, that, as you see, will not spill much blood. (*The children burst out a-laughing.*)

FRANK (*in apology*).—My lord, I spoke a little bluntly.

LORD CARLTON (*to Frank*).—You are an excellent young

gentleman, and deserve much better than he does, to wear this badge of honor. As a token of my esteem and acknowledgment, accept this sword ; but I will first put a blade to it that may be worthy of you. (*He pulls from under his coat the proper blade.*)

FRANK.—Your lordship is too good ; but allow us to withdraw.

LORD CARLTON.—No, no, my dear boys, you shall stay. Come with me into another apartment. As for you, sir, (*to Augustus*) do not offer to stir from this place. You may celebrate your birthday here all alone. You shall never wear a sword again until you deserve one. (*He goes out followed by the boys. Augustus slinks along opposite side and then out.*)

FAUNTLEROY AND THE EARL.

Adapted by Mr. H. Q. Emery, from "Little Lord Fauntleroy," by Mrs. Frances Hodgson Burnett.

CHARACTERS.

Earl of Dorincourt, *a very tall, straight man, with hooked nose and white hair.*

Lord Fauntleroy, *a beautiful little boy of seven, with light curly hair—grandson to the Earl.*

A Footman.

Situation.—LITTLE LORD FAUNTLEROY'S *father married in America, was disinherited by the* EARL, *and not long after died. The* EARL'S *other sons died without children, and so the* EARL *relented and sent for* LITTLE LORD FAUNTLEROY, *as he was then to be called.*

The following dialogue is the first appearance of the little boy before his grandfather. His mother, whom he calls DEAREST *lives at the Lodge just outside the park in which the* EARL'S *castle is located.*

The EARL *has deep, fierce eyes, and a harsh voice. He is a cruel, hard-hearted man, who suffers from the gout.* FAUNTLEROY *is an exceedingly lovable little fellow of the utmost courage and innocence. He is dressed in a black velvet suit, with a large lace collar, and with a sash at his waist. He believes in everybody and thinks everyone trusts him.*

53

The dialogue takes place in the library of Dorincourt Castle, a large room with massive furniture in it and shelves of books.

Enter the EARL OF DORINCOURT, *walking with difficulty, and using a cane. He comes down and sits beside table, putting his gouty foot on foot-rest; he speaks as he comes down.*

EARL OF DORINCOURT.—All done for effect! She thinks I shall admire her spirit! I don't admire it! It's only American independence! I won't have her living like a beggar at my park gates. As she's the boy's mother she has a position to keep up, and she shall keep it up. She shall have the money whether she likes it or not. She shan't tell people that she has to live like a pauper because I have done nothing for her. She wants to give the boy a bad opinion of me!

Enter FOOTMAN.

FOOTMAN (*with a bow*).—Lord Fauntleroy, my lord. (*He goes out on other side.*)

Enter LORD FAUNTLEROY. *He comes slowly down, looking all around him until he discovers the Earl.*

FAUNTLEROY.—How do you do? Are you the Earl? I'm your grandson, you know, that Mr. Havisham brought. I'm Lord Fauntleroy. (*Holds out his hand.*) I hope you are very well. I'm very glad to see you.

(*The Earl shakes hands, after looking him over from head to foot.*)

EARL OF DORINCOURT.—Glad to see me, are you?

FAUNTLEROY.—Yes, very. (*He sits in chair the other side of table and looks at the Earl.*) I've kept wondering what you would look like. I used to lie in my berth in the ship and wonder if you would be anything like my father.

EARL OF DORINCOURT.—Am I?

FAUNTLEROY.—Well, I was very young when he died, and I may not remember exactly how he looked, but I don't think you are like him.

EARL OF DORINCOURT.—You are disappointed, I suppose?

FAUNTLEROY.—Oh, no; of course you would like any one to look like your father, but of course you would enjoy the way your grandfather looked, even if he wasn't like your father. You know how it is yourself about admiring your relations. (*The Earl leans back and stares at him.*)

FAUNTLEROY.—Any boy would love his grandfather. Especially one that had been as kind to him as you have been.

EARL OF DORINCOURT.—Oh, I have been kind to you, have I?

FAUNTLEROY.—Yes; I'm ever so much obliged to you about Bridget, and the apple-woman, and Dick.

EARL OF DORINCOURT.—Bridget! Dick! The apple-woman!

FAUNTLEROY.—Yes, the ones you gave me all that money for—the money you told Mr. Havisham to give me.

EARL OF DORINCOURT.—Ha! That's it, is it? The money you were to spend as you liked. What did you buy with it?

FAUNTLEROY.—Well, you see, Michael had the fever.

EARL OF DORINCOURT.—Who's Michael?

FAUNTLEROY.—Michael's Bridget's husband, and they were in great trouble. When a man's sick and can't work, and has twelve children, you know how it is. And Bridget used to come to our house and cry, and I went in to see her, and Mr. Havisham sent for me and he said you had given him some money for me. And I ran as fast as I could and gave it to Bridget and that made it all right. That's why I'm so obliged to you.

EARL OF DORINCOURT.—Oh! That was one of the things you did for yourself, was it? What else?

FAUNTLEROY.—Well, there was Dick. You'd like Dick. He's so square.

EARL OF DORINCOURT.—What does that mean?

FAUNTLEROY (*thoughtfully*).—I think it means he wouldn't cheat anybody, or hit a boy who was under his size, and that he blacks people's boots very well and makes them shine as much as he can. He's a professional bootblack.

EARL OF DORINCOURT.—And he's one of your acquaintances, is he?

FAUNTLEROY.—He's an old friend of mine. Not quite as old as Mr. Hobbs, but quite old. (*The Earl looks at him in bewilderment.*)—You don't wear your coronet all the time?

EARL OF DORINCOURT.—No, it is not becoming to me.

FAUNTLEROY.—Mr. Hobbs said you always wore it; but after he thought it over he said he supposed you must sometimes take it off to put your hat on.

EARL OF DORINCOURT (*he gives a sharp glance at him and a half laugh*).—Yes, I take it off occasionally.

FAUNTLEROY (*looks around room*).—You must be very proud of your house, it's such a beautiful house. I never saw anything so beautiful, but of course as I'm only seven, I haven't seen much.

EARL OF DORINCOURT.—And you think I should be very proud, do you?

FAUNTLEROY.—I should be proud of it if it were my house. Everything about it is beautiful. It's a very big house for just two people to live in, isn't it?

EARL OF DORINCOURT.—It is quite large enough for two. Do you find it too large?

FAUNTLEROY (*hesitates*).—I was only thinking that if two people lived in it who were not very good companions they might feel lonely sometimes.

EARL OF DORINCOURT.—Do you think I shall make a good companion?

FAUNTLEROY.—Yes. I think you will. Mr. Hobbs and I were great friends. He was the best friend I had except Dearest.

EARL OF DORINCOURT (*lifts eyebrows*).—Who is Dearest?

FAUNTLEROY.—She is my mother. (*He sighs.*) I—I think I'd better get up and walk up and down the room. (*He does so with his hands in his pockets.*)

EARL OF DORINCOURT (*watching him a moment or two*).—Come here.

FAUNTLEROY (*goes to him*).—I never was away from my own house before. It makes a person have a strange feeling when he has to stay all night in another person's castle instead of his own house. But Dearest is not very far away from me.

EARL OF DORINCOURT (*knits his brow, then looks at Fauntleroy*).—I suppose you think you are fond of her.

FAUNTLEROY.—Yes. I do think so and I think it's true. My father left her to me to take care of and when I'm a man I am going to work and earn money for her.

EARL OF DORINCOURT.—What do you think of doing?

FAUNTLEROY.—I did think of going into business with Mr. Hobbs; but I should *like* to be a President.

EARL OF DORINCOURT.—We'll send you to the House of Lords instead.

FAUNTLEROY.—Well, if I couldn't be a President, and if

that is a good business, I shouldn't mind. The grocery business is dull sometimes.

Enter FOOTMAN.

FOOTMAN.—Dinner is served, my lord.

FAUNTLEROY (*looks at Earl's foot*).—Would you like me to help you? You could lean on me, you know. Once Mr. Hobbs hurt his foot with a potato barrel rolling on it, and he used to lean on me.

EARL OF DORINCOURT (*looks at him a moment*).—Do you think you could do it.

FAUNTLEROY.—I *think* I could. I'm seven, you know. You could lean on your stick on one side, and Dick says I've a good deal of muscle for a boy of seven. (*He doubles up his arm to show his muscle.*)

EARL OF DORINCOURT (*waves footman away*).—Well, you may try. (*Gets up and puts hand on Fauntleroy's shoulder.*)

FAUNTLEROY.—Don't be afraid of leaning on me, I'm all right—if—if it isn't a very long way. (*They slowly go up the room, the boy staggering under the Earl's weight.*) Does your foot hurt you very much when you stand on it ? Did you ever put it in hot water and mustard ? Mr. Hobbs used to put his in hot water. Arnica is a very nice thing, they tell me.

EARL OF DORINCOURT.—No, I never tried hot water. Pretty heavy, am I not?

FAUNTLEROY.—Well, a little ; but I'm all right. Lean on me, grandfather—just lean on me. (*Both go out. Footman has stood at back trying not to laugh, and now goes out after them with a gesture of mirthful despair.*)

THE RECONCILIATION.

Adapted from " Little Women," by Louise M. Alcott.

CHARACTERS.

Mr. Lawrence, *an old bald-headed man of irritable temper, with spectacles on.*

Teddy Lawrence, *called* LAURIE, *his grandson.*

Josephine Marsh, *called* Jo, *a girl with short hair.*

Situation.—LAURIE *has written letters to* MEG *and so caused considerable trouble. He has implicated* Jo, *whose mother has called in all the children concerned, found out the truth and enjoined strict secrecy on all.* LAURIE'S *grandfather has tried in vain to find out his escapade and has threatened to punish him. So* LAURIE *has gone to his room to plan to run away.* Jo *pacifies him and then his grandfather, and then goes home.*

Scene I.

LAURIE *sits sulkily at his table, with his head resting on his hands. There is a smart rap at the door.*

LAURIE (*in a threatening tone*).—Stop that, or I'll open the door and make you. (*The knocking is repeated immediately. He goes to the door, opens it quickly and in bounces Jo. He strides across the room.*)

Jo (*dropping down artistically on her knees*).—Please forgive me for being so cross. I came to make it up, and can't go away till I have.

59

LAURIE (*with great show of wisdom*).—It's all right. Get up, and don't be a goose, Jo.

Jo (*rising*).—Thank you; I will. Could I ask what's the matter? You don't look exactly easy in your mind.

LAURIE (*indignantly*).—I've been shaken and I won't bear it.

Jo.—Who did it?

LAURIE.—Grandfather; if it had been any one else I'd have—(*an energetic gesture of his right arm.*)

Jo (*soothingly*).—That's nothing; I often shake you, and you don't mind.

LAURIE.—Pooh! you're a girl, and it's fun; but I'll allow no man to shake *me*.

Jo.—I don't think any one would care to try it, if you looked as much like a thunder-cloud as you do now. Why were you treated so?

LAURIE.—Just because I wouldn't say what your mother wanted me for. I'd promised not to tell, and of course I wasn't going to break my word.

Jo.—Couldn't you satisfy your grandpa in any other way?

LAURIE.—No; he *would* have the truth, the whole truth, and nothing but the truth. I'd have told my part of the scrape, if I could without bringing Meg in. As I couldn't, I held my tongue, and bore the scolding till the old gentleman collared me. Then I got angry, and bolted, for fear I should forget myself.

Jo.—It wasn't nice, but he's sorry, I know; so go down and make up. I'll help you.

LAURIE.—Hanged if I do! I'm not going to be lectured and pummelled by every one, just for a bit of a frolic. I *was* sorry about Meg, and begged pardon like a man; but I won't do it again, when I wasn't in the wrong.

Jo.—He didn't know that.

LAURIE.—He ought to trust me, and not act as if I was a baby. It's no use, Jo; he's got to learn that I'm able to take care of myself, and don't need any one's apron-string to hold on by.

Jo (*with a sigh*).—What pepper-pots you are! How do you mean to settle this affair?

LAURIE.—Well, he ought to beg pardon, and believe me when I say I can't tell him what the fuss's about.

Jo.—Bless you! he won't do that.

LAURIE.—I won't go down till he does.

Jo.—Now, Teddy, be sensible; let it pass, and I'll explain what I can. You can't stay here, so what's the use of being melodramatic?

LAURIE.—I don't intend to stay here long anyway. I'll slip off and take a journey somewhere, and when grandpa misses me he'll come round fast enough.

Jo.—I daresay; but you ought not to go and worry him.

LAURIE.—Don't preach. I'll go to Washington and see Brooke. It's gay there, and I'll enjoy myself after the troubles.

Jo *forgetting herself in the prospect*).—What fun you'd have! I wish I could run off too.

LAURIE.—Come on, then! Why not? You go and surprise your father there, and I'll stir up old Brooke. It would be a glorious joke; let's do it, Jo. We'll leave a letter saying we are all right, and trot off at once. I've got money enough; it will do you good; and be no harm, as you go to your father.

Jo (*looking wistfully out of the window*).—If I was a boy, we'd run away together, and have a capital time; but as I'm a miserable girl, I must be proper, and stop at home. Don't tempt me, Teddy, it's a crazy plan.

LAURIE.—That's the fun of it——

Jo (*covering her ears*).—Hold your tongue ! " Prunes and prisms " are my doom, and I may as well make up my mind to it. I came here to moralize, not to hear about things that make me skip to think of.

LAURIE (*insinuatingly*).—I know Meg would wet-blanket such a proposal, but I thought you had more spirit.

Jo.—Bad boy, be quiet ! Sit down and think of your own sins, don't go making me add to mine. If I get your grandpa to apologize for the shaking, will you give up running away?

LAURIE.—Yes,—but you won't do it.

Jo (*to herself as she goes out*).—If I can manage the young one I can the old one. (*Laurie pulls out a railroad map and studies it as curtain goes down.*)

Scene II.

A library. MR. LAWRENCE *is seated by a table with books on it. There is a high bookcase and, in another part of the room, high steps.* Jo *taps at the door.*

MR. LAWRENCE (*gruffly*).—Come in !

Jo *enters.*

Jo (*blandly*).—It's only me, sir, come to return a book.

MR. LAWRENCE (*grimly*).—Want any more?

Jo (*trying to please him*).—Yes, please. I like Old Sam so well I think I'll try the second volume. (*Mr. Lawrence places the steps so as to reach the books and Jo skips up them, and perches on the top step, where she looks the books over.*)

MR. LAWRENCE (*walking about the room*).—What has that boy been about? Don't try to shield him. I know he has been in mischief by the way he acted when he came home. I can't get a word from him ; and when I threatened to shake the truth out of him he bolted upstairs, and locked himself into his room.

Jo (*reluctantly*).—He did do wrong but we forgave him, and all promised not to say a word to any one.

MR. LAWRENCE.—That won't do; he shall not shelter himself behind a promise from you soft-hearted girls. If he's done anything amiss, he shall confess, beg pardon, and be punished. Out with it, Jo, I won't be kept in the dark.

Jo (*looking a little frightened*).—Indeed, sir, I cannot tell; mother forbade it. Laurie has confessed, asked pardon, and been punished quite enough. We don't keep silence to shield him, but some one else, and it will make more trouble if you interfere. Please don't; it was partly my fault, but it's all right now; so let's forget it, and talk about the " Rambler," or something pleasant.

MR. LAWRENCE.—Hang the " Rambler ! " Come down and give me your word that this harum-scarum boy of mine hasn't done anything ungrateful or impertinent. If he has, after all your kindness to him, I'll thrash him with my own hands.

Jo (*descending very cheerfully*).—Well, there were some letters written, and they were answered, and then we found out it wasn't the person we supposed, but some one else, and then everybody promised mother not to say anything about—and that's all.

MR. LAWRENCE (*rubbing up his hair till it stands on end*). —Hum—ha—well, if the boy held his tongue because he promised, and not from obstinacy, I'll forgive him. He's a stubborn fellow, and hard to manage.

Jo (*courageously*).—So am I ; but a kind word will govern me when all the king's horses and all the king's men couldn't.

MR. LAWRENCE (*sharply*).—You think I'm not kind to him, then?

JO.—Oh, dear, no, sir; You are rather too kind sometimes, and then just a trifle hasty when he tries your patience. Don't you think you are?

MR. LAWRENCE (*throwing his spectacles on the table*).— You're right, girl, I am! I love the boy, but he tries my patience past bearing, and I don't know how it will end, if we go on so.

JO.—I'll tell you. He'll run away. (*Mr. Lawrence looks troubled and sits down.*) He won't do it unless he is very much worried, and only threatens it sometimes, when he gets tired of studying. I often think I should like to, especially since my hair was cut; (*laughing*) so, if you ever miss us, you may advertise for two boys, and look among the ships bound for India.

MR. LAWRENCE (*relieved*).—You hussy, how dare you talk in that way? Where's your respect for me, and your proper bringing up? Bless the boys and girls! (*He pinches her cheeks.*) What torments they are; yet we can't do without them. Go and bring that boy down to his dinner, tell him it's all right, and advise him not to put on tragedy airs with his grandfather. I won't bear it.

JO (*trying to look pathetic*).—He won't come, sir; he feels badly because you didn't believe him when he said he couldn't tell. I think the shaking hurt his feelings very much.

MR. LAWRENCE (*laughing*).—I'm sorry for that, and ought to thank him for not shaking *me*, I suppose. What the dickens does the fellow expect?

JO (*looking wise*).—If I were you, I'd write him an apology, sir. He says he won't come down till he has one, and talks about Washington, and goes on in an absurd way. A formal apology will make him see how foolish he is, and bring him down quite amiable. Try it; he likes fun, and this way is better than talking. I'll carry it up, and teach him his duty.

MR. LAWRENCE (*gives her a sharp look, then puts on his spectacles and writes*).—You're a sly puss, but I don't mind being managed by you and Beth. Here, give me a bit of paper, and let us have done with this nonsense. (*He writes and folds the note, while Jo watches him. She drops a kiss on his bald head, takes the note and goes out.*)

Scene III.

A hallway before LAURIE'S *chamber door.*

Jo *enters and knocks on the door.*

Jo (*slips the note under the door and talks through the keyhole*).—Here is the apology. You're expected down to dinner, and you must act submissive and decorous, and not be foolish. (*She tries the door, finds it locked and starts away.*)

LAURIE *comes out, laughing.*

LAURIE.—What a good fellow you are, Jo! Did you get blown up?

Jo.—No, he was pretty mild on the whole.

LAURIE.—Ah! I got it all round. Even you cast me off over there, and I felt just ready to go to the deuce.

Jo.—Don't talk in that way; turn over a new leaf and begin again, Teddy, my son.

LAURIE (*dolefully*).—I keep turning over new leaves, and spoiling them, as I used to spoil my copy-books; and I make so many beginnings there never will be an end.

Jo.—Go and eat your dinner; you'll feel better after it. Men always croak when they are hungry. (*She hurries out.*)

LAURIE.—That's a "label" on my "sect." (*He goes out.*)

5

KEEPING HOUSE.

CHARACTERS.

Lizzie Merriam, *a haughty overbearing girl, who wears large rings and a coral necklace.*

Bessie Belmont, *a polite but ambitious girl, who wants to lead others.*

Lucy Dawson, *a quiet girl who loves the truth.*

Mary Dawson, *a sick little girl, who always lies on the sofa.*

Polly Dawson, *a little child full of mischief, who carries a case knife.*

Situation.—BESSIE, *a cousin, and* LIZZIE, *a neighbor, come to play with the* DAWSON *children.* MARY *has fallen down-stairs and injured her leg so she has to have a splint on it, and she is confined to her room. All the girls go there to play. They pretend to keep house until* LIZZIE, *provoked because* LUCY *says she ate up the cake, flies into a passion and rushes home.*

On one side of the platform is a sofa; on the other is a screen behind which is a table partially set with doll's dishes. The platform is otherwise furnished as a sitting room.

MARY *lies on the sofa.* LUCY *enters quietly.*

LUCY.—Mamma says we can play in your room this afternoon.

MARY.—Well, I'm glad, 'cause you haven't played up here for three days.

LUCY.—What shall we play when they come?

66

MARY.—Who's a-comin' 'cept Polly and you?

LUCY.—Why, Bessie said she would come over, if Aunt Jane would let her, and perhaps Lizzie Merriam will come. (*A noise without.*)

MARY.—Well, I guess they've all of 'em come by the sound.

LUCY (*she opens the door*).—Yes, here's Bessie and Polly and Lizzie.

Enter BESSIE, POLLY *and* LIZZIE.

MARY.—I'm glad to see you all and I think it would be very nice to play house.

BESSIE.—Yes, and then you can take part, too.

LIZZIE.—I will be the lady of the house, because I have rings on my fingers and a coral necklace.—My name is Mrs. Sprat. Mary, you shall be Mrs. Gobang, come a-visiting me; because you can't do anything else. We'll make believe you've lost your husband in the wars. I know a Mrs. Gobang, she is always *taking-on* just this way, and saying, "My poor dear husband!" (*She says the words with a very nasal twang behind her handkerchief, and they all laugh.*)

LUCY.—Well, what shall I be?

LIZZIE.—Oh, you shall be a hired girl, and wear a hand-kerchief on your head, just as our girl does. And you must be a little deaf and keep saying "What, ma'am?" when I speak to you.

BESSIE.—And I will be Mr. Jack Sprat, the head of the family.

LIZZIE.—Yes, you can put on a waterproof cloak, and you will make quite a good-looking husband; but I shall be the head of the family myself, and have things about as I please.

BESSIE (*putting on her cloak*).—Well, there, I don't know about that; I don't think it's very polite for you to treat your husband in that way.

LIZZIE (*with a toss of the head*).—But I believe in "Woman's Rights" and if there's anything I despise, it is a *man* meddling about the house.

LUCY (*to Polly, who is hitting a knife she has stuck into a crack in a chair, and making a whirring noise*).—I wouldn't do so, Polly, it troubles us, and besides I'm afraid it will break the knife.

LIZZIE (*as Mrs Sprat*).—I don't allow my hired girl to interfere with my children. I am mistress of the house, I'd have you to know. There, little daughter, they shan't plague her. She shall keep on doing mischief, so she shall. (*Polly redoubles her efforts with the knife.*)

MARY (*groaning loudly*).—Oh! oh! oh! My poor husband! all dead of a cannon-bullet! Oh! oh!

LIZZIE (*trying to make conversation*).—My good Mrs. Gobang, I think I have got something in my eye; will you please tell me how it looks?

MARY (*looking into it*).—Oh, your eye looks very well, ma'am. Don't 'xcuse it, it looks well enough for *me*.

LIZZIE.—Ahem! (*She arranges her dress.*) Are your feet warm, Mrs. Gobang?

MARY.—Thank you, ma'am I don't feel 'em cold. Oh, dear, if your husband was all deaded up, I guess you'd cry, Mrs. Sprat. (*She weeps into her handkerchief.*)

LIZZIE (*with a threatening gesture*).—You must go right out of the parlor, Bridget. I mean you, Lucy,——the parlor isn't any place for hired girls.

LUCY (*inclining her head*).—Ma'am?

LIZZIE (*moaning*).—Oh, dear, the plague of having a deaf girl! You don't know how trying it is, Mrs. Gobang!

That hired girl, Bridget, hears with her elbows, Mrs. Gobang, I verily believe she does.

MARY.—Oh, no, ma'am, I guess she doesn't hear with
her elbows, does she? If she *heard* with her elbows, she
wouldn't have to ask you over again. (*Every one laughs
and Lucy looks at her elbows*).—Will you please, ma'am,
ask Bridget to *hot* a flatiron? I've cried my handkerchief
all up.

LIZZIE.—Yes, go right out, Bridget and *hot* a flatiron.
Go out, this instant, and build a fire, Bridget.

BESSIE (*as Mr. Sprat*).—Yes, go right out, Bridget.
(*Lucy goes out.*)

MARY (*sobbing as Mrs. Gobang*).—It was my darlin'
husband's handkerchief.

BESSIE (*laughing*).—Rather a small one for a man.

MARY (*quickly*).—Well, my husband had a very small
nose.

LIZZIE (*as Mrs. Sprat*).—Oh, Mrs. Gobang, you ought
to be exceeding thankful you're a widow, and don't keep
house. I think my hired girls will carry down my gray
hairs to the grave. The last one I had was Irish and very
Catholic. (*Mary groans and looks for a dry spot on her
handkerchief.*) Yes, indeed it was awful, for she was always going to masses and mass-meetings. And there
couldn't anybody die but they must be "waked" you
know.

MARY (*opened her eyes*).—Why, I didn't know they
could be waked up when they was dead.

LIZZIE.—Oh, but they only *make believe* you can wake
'em; of course it isn't true. For my part, I don't believe
a word an Irish girl says, any way. (*Polly who has at in-
tervals kept up a noise with the knife now makes a scrap-
ing, rasping sound*).—Bridget, Bridget!

LUCY *enters.*

Lucy (*bending her head to one side*).—Ma'am?

Lizzie.—Why in the world don't you see to that baby? I believe you are losing your mind.

Lucy.—Ma'am?

Lizzie.—Take her out! (*Lucy takes Polly out.*)

Mary.—That makes me think. What do you s'pose the reason is folks can't be waked up? What makes 'em stay in heaven all the days, and nights and years, and never come down here to see anybody, not a minute?

Lizzie.—What an idea! I'm sure I don't know.

Mary.—Well, I've been a thinkin', that when God has sended 'em up to the sky, they like to stay up there the best. It's a nicer place, a great deal nicer place, up in God's house.

Lizzie.—Oh, yes, of course, but our play——

Mary.—I've been a-thinkin' that when I go up to God's house, I sha'n't wear the splint. I can run all over the house, and he'll be willing I should go upstairs; and down cellar, you know. (*She sighs.*)

Lizzie (*impatiently*).—Well, let's go on with our play. It's most supper-time, Mrs. Gobang. Come in, Bridget.

LUCY *enters.*

Lucy (*turning up one ear*).—Ma'am?

Lizzie.—Bridget, have you attended to your sister—to my little child, I mean? (*Lucy nods.*) Then go out and make some sassafras-cakes, and some eel-pie, and some squirrel-soup. And set the table in five minutes do you hear?

Lucy.—Ma'am, what did you say about gingerbread?

Bessie (*as Mr. Sprat*).—Oh, how stupid Bridget is!

Mrs. Sprat says eel-jumbles, and sassafras-pie, and pound-cake, all made in five minutes. (*Everybody laughs.*)

MARY (*sighing*).—Oh, my darlin' husband used to like jumble-pie. I've forgot to cry for ever so long. (*She weeps and turns away her head.*)

LUCY (*she has moved the table into the middle of the floor and gone out. She now returns*).—Please, ma'am. I just made some eel-jumbles and things, and a dog came in and stole them.

LIZZIE.—Very well, Bridget, make some more.

BESSIE.—Yes, make some more, and chain up that dog.

LUCY.—But real honest true, the fruit-cake *is* all gone out of our play chest. You ate it up, you know, Lizzie. But it's no matter. We'll cut up some cookies, or may be mother 'll let us have some oyster-crackers.

LIZZIE (*angrily*).—*I* ate up the cake ! It's no such thing, I never touched it !

LUCY.—Oh, but you did. I suppose you've forgotten. You went to the cake-chest this morning, and last night, and yesterday noon, and ever so many more times. (*Lizzie cannot speak from anger.*)—But it's just as well. You could have it as well as not, and perfectly welcome.

LIZZIE (*indignantly*).—What are you talking about? I wonder if you take me for a pig, Lucy Dawson? I heard what your mother said about that cake. She said it was too dry for her company, but it was too rich for little girls, and we must only eat a *teeny* speck at a time. I told my mamma and she laughed, to think such mean dried-up cake was too rich for little girls !

LUCY.—It *was* rich, nice cake, Lizzie, but mother said the slices had been cut a great while, and it was drying up. Let's not talk any more about it.

LIZZIE.—Oh, but I shall talk more about it. You keep

hinting that I tell wrong stories and steal victuals. Yes you do! And you ain't willing to let me speak. (*There is a slight pause for a reply but Lucy says nothing; so Lizzie rises.*) I won't stay here to be imposed upon, and told that I'm a liar and a thief, so I won't! I'll go right home this very minute, and tell my mother just how you treat your company! (*She flounces out of the room in great anger.*)

LUCY (*following her to the door*).—Oh, don't go, Lizzie. Stay and play!

BESSIE (*coolly, as the door slams*).—Well, I'm glad she's gone. She's a bold thing, and my mother wouldn't like me to play with her, if she knew how she acts. She said " victuals " for food and that isn't *elegant*, mother says. What right had she to set up and say she'd be Mrs. Sprat? So forward!

LUCY.—But I'm *sorry* she's gone. I don't like to have her go and tell that I wasn't polite.

MARY.—You *was* polite, a great deal politer'n she was. I wouldn't care if I would be you, Lucy. I don't wish Lizzie was dead, but I wish she was a duck a-sailin' on the water!

CURTAIN.

THE LOST PRINCESS.

CHARACTERS.

Miss Amelia, *a tall, middle-aged lady, kindly but precise.*

Viola Lea, *a beautiful young girl, with black hair and large dark eyes, dressed in white.*

Uncle Wise, *an old white-headed negro, body-servant to* HENRY LEA, *of the South.*

Dr. Elliot Barber, *a fine-looking young man, physician to* MISS AMELIA'S *household.*

Aunt Bess, *a young lady of beauty, aunt to* VIOLA LEA, *engaged to* DR. BARBER.

Two servants.

Situation.—*Little* VIOLA LEA, *lost in the cemetery at her grandfather's funeral, has been brought into* MISS AMELIA'S *presence. The only one who can identify her is* UNCLE WISE, *an old servant of her grandfather's. His story reminds* DR. BARBER *that his fiancée is searching for just such a little wanderer. So* VIOLA *is recognized as a stolen niece and henceforth finds a home.*

MISS AMELIA *enters, leading* VIOLA *by the hand. She sits down and puts her arm around the little girl.*

MISS AMELIA.—Are you lost, dear child?

73

VIOLA.—Yes, yes!

MISS AMELIA.—Where do you live?

VIOLA.—I can't think of *where* now. We have been there five days, Grandpa, Uncle Wise, and I.

MISS AMELIA.—What is your name, dear?

VIOLA.—I was papa's "Little Princess," but I am Grand-papa's "Viola Lea." Oh, but now that he is dead, I suppose I am just Uncle Wise's "Little Mistress." I belong now just to him. But that can't be either, for he says he belongs to me.

MISS AMELIA.—Why did Uncle Wise allow you to go out all alone?

VIOLA (*plaintively*). — Oh, he took the fever, too! (*Earnestly.*) And I ought to go back to him now, poor old Uncle Wise. But may I have some water first? I am so thirsty.

MISS AMELIA.—Certainly, little one, you shall have all the water you want. (*Enter servant with a letter which she hands to Miss Amelia.*) Give this little girl a drink of water and bring her back to me. (*The servant goes out with Viola.*) (*She opens letter.*) Oh, from Dr. Barber! (*She reads.*) "There is an old colored man going about from house to house in the city, inquiring for a little girl named Viola Lea. Hearing that a child had been found near the cemetery and brought to you, I have sent him out to you."

Enter SERVANT.

SERVANT.—There is a colored man downstairs, ma'am, who wants to see you very particular.

MISS AMELIA.—Send him up. I will see him here.

Re-enter VIOLA *on one side and* UNCLE WISE *with servant on the other side. Servant goes out.* VIOLA *and* UNCLE

WISE *meet near the centre of platform, while* MISS
AMELIA *withdraws a little to one side.*

UNCLE WISE.—Why, little mistes, honey, you has given
ole Uncle Wise a heap o' trouble. I's looked fur you high
an' low all over dis big town. Why'd you go to yo' Grandpa's funeral when I wuz too sick to go with you? Who
tuk you thar, anyhow, little Miss?

VIOLA.—Oh, I wanted to see where they put poor Grand-
papa and I begged the man who drove Grandpa to take
me up on the seat with him and he let me come. He was
ever so kind.

UNCLE WISE.—But why didn't you ride back with him?

VIOLA.—Oh, I wandered around looking at the flowers
and got lost. I think I must have fallen asleep because I
woke up and felt very hungry.

MISS AMELIA (*rings the bell and a servant enters*).—Here,
my dear, go with the servant and eat all you want while I
talk a little with Uncle Wise. (*Viola, looking very much
exhausted, follows servant out. Miss Amelia turns toward
Uncle Wise*). Now, tell me who the child is and who her
family are?

UNCLE WISE (*standing and twirling his hat*).—Well, now,
marm, dat's what I can't tell you.

MISS AMELIA.—Why not? Do you not know?

UNCLE WISE.—Yes, marm, I knows, but——(*he puts his
hand to his head, sinks to a chair and falls to thinking,
while Miss Amelia watches him.*)

MISS AMELIA (*rings a bell and a servant appears*).—Go
bring the Doctor. I fear the poor old man is ill.

SERVANT.—He was downstairs just now talking to that
little girl.

MISS AMELIA.—Ask him to come up at once. (*The
servant goes out.*)

UNCLE WISE.—Will my little lady be back soon? I want her to come with me.

MISS AMELIA.—Go with *you!* Do you think that you, an old colored man, are the proper person to have the care of this child? She shall not leave my house until I deliver her to her relations.

UNCLE WISE.—Well, lady, the good Lord's will be done; but de marster, her grandfather, would have trusted her with me to de ends of de earth.

Enter DOCTOR.

DOCTOR.—Ah, Miss Amelia, this is Uncle Wise, I take it. (*He looks at Uncle Wise keenly.*) Still got a little fever about you, I see.

UNCLE WISE.—Yes, seh, I'm gettin' ole an' am gwine to de blessed home pretty soon, I reckon.

MISS AMELIA.—Doctor, do get him to tell us everything about the child.

DOCTOR (*drawing a chair near to Uncle Wise*).—Do you hear, Uncle Wise? She wishes you to tell us of the relations of your little mistress.

UNCLE WISE.—Yes, seh, that is whut I'm minded to do. I'm feelin' mighty weak an' troubled in my mine 'bout the chile.

DOCTOR.—Well, then, begin immediately.

UNCLE WISE.—I wuz a-thinkin' that I might begin when Marse Henry an' me wuz boys. I like to think of dat good time.

DOCTOR.—No. That was before the war, and you are not strong. Begin after the war.

UNCLE WISE.—Well, now, let me see. Did I tell you 'bout when Marse Henry an' his daughter Edith an' me went to Europe?

DOCTOR.—No. You have told us nothing.

UNCLE WISE.—Well, we did go to Europe, dat's de point, dat's whar de trouble wuz. Marster, he wuz so 'pressed, totin' his head so low after his mother an' Miss Viola, his wife, died, dat he 'lowed he couldn't go back to de ole place an' see they empty cheers. So we went to Europe. Miss Edith wuz 'bout sixteen years ole den. She sut'n'y wuz mighty pretty, but with a sot will of her own like her pa. She liked Paris de mos' an' so her pa left her thar to study fur a year. But when we got back to Paris, little miss was gone. She'd done married de han'somest gent'-man in de worl' an' run off with him to his home in Italy. Marster, he stormed an' raged, an' when he hurd she married a po' 'Talian prince, he stormed mo' an' mo', an' raged red-hot. I thought he'd jes bu'n up.

DOCTOR.—Did your master try to find his daughter?

UNCLE WISE (*shaking his head*).—'Bout a year after dis we hurd how Miss Edith had a fine dorter, an' dat they had christened her Viola Lea. One day thar come a telegraph from Naples, sayin', "Edith is dead." (*The Doctor seems to recognize the story.*)

MISS AMELIA.—Well, well, go on. Did you go to Naples?

UNCLE WISE.—Yes, marm, we went. An' every day marster went to de park an' sot under a tree an' watched a young lady an' a little girl, ez alway come ev'y day to walk in dat park. So, soon I make out whut marster knowed all along, dat dis here pretty little girl wuz Miss Edith's baby, an' de young lady, whut they call Miss Eliza-beth wuz a sister of dat dar prince.

DOCTOR (*much agitated*).—I have some important mat-ters to attend to and—you will excuse me, Miss Amelia, for a short while. (*He goes out.*)

MISS AMELIA.—Will you proceed, Uncle Wise?

UNCLE WISE.—One day while de young lady talked to a officer in de park, marster an' me tuck de little girl an' 'scaped with her to France, an' den to England. The little girl—dat's de one you have.

MISS AMELIA.—What! Stole the child!

UNCLE WISE (*falteringly*).—No. Not zackely. We jes tuck yer. She belonged one-half to Marse Henry, bein' as she wuz a Lea, Miss Edith's chile.

MISS AMELIA.—Why, I don't see how, you can call it anything else but stealing. (*She rises and walks about.*)

UNCLE WISE.—De good Lord forgive me if I stole her, I dat wouldn't steal even a mushmelon. Lord, how I's come in thy sight! (*Covers his face with his hands and goes out.*)

Enter VIOLA.

VIOLA.—Where is Uncle Wise?

MISS AMELIA.—He will be right back.

DOCTOR *and* MISS ELIZABETH *enter.*

AUNT BESS (*rushing over to Viola and holding out her hand*).—Don't you know me, Viola? Don't you remember Aunt Bess?

VIOLA (*slowly*).—No, I do not remember. But I think I would like to remember you. Are you really my own Aunt Bess? (*She comes close, leans forward, with both hands pinches Aunt Bess's cheeks, and kisses her quickly on the lips.*)

AUNT BESS (*clasping Viola in her arms and turning to the Doctor*).—O, Elliott, it is the same little kiss I taught her when she was but three years old—our baby's " French kiss."

VIOLA.—And may I stay here, always, with you, Aunt Bess an Miss Amelia?

AUNT BESS.—Yes, my darling, you shan't leave us any more.

VIOLA.—Oh, I shall be so happy, then, always if only poor old Uncle Wise could stay here too.

DOCTOR.—He may, we will not send him away, knowing that this would make our little Princess unhappy.

SELLING THE IMAGE.

Adapted from " Toinette's Philip," by Mrs. C. V. Jamison.

CHARACTERS.

Mr. Ainsworth, *a prosperous artist.*

Philip, *a handsome boy, with large blue eyes and curling brown hair; he wears a blue shirt and blue trousers, and a white cap; he carries a tray of flowers.*

Dea, *a small girl, in a long dark-red frock; a long white muslin scarf round her neck crosses on her breast, is tied behind her back and falls almost to the ground; a red silk handkerchief covers her head and is knotted under her chin; a covered basket is on her arm.*

Seline, *a large, good-natured colored woman; she wears a white apron and cap.*

Situation.—SELINE *sells fruit and nuts on a street corner in New Orleans. Two waifs,* PHILIP *and* DEA, *interest her.* PHILIP *sells flowers;* DEA *sells little wax images made by her poor and eccentric father.* SELINE *has been away for some weeks and the children have not had good fortune.* SELINE *decides to help* DEA *sell her images and so interests* MR. AINSWORTH, *who pays the price asked and negotiates for more.* DEA'S *quaint* *figure appeals to his artistic instincts and* PHILIP *looks like his dead son.*

DEA *carries in her basket two figures, Esmeralda and her goat, and Quasimodo, the hunchback of Notre Dame,—characters in Victor Hugo's great novel, Notre Dame. A wolf-dog follows the children as they enter, and lies down under* SELINE'S *stand.*

A street corner. SELINE *is behind her stand, when* PHILIP *and* DEA *come rushing in.*

DEA.—Yes, there she is ! (*She runs to her arms.*)

SELINE (*clasping the child*).—Oh, honey, how glad I is ter see yer—an' Mars' Philip, too !—how you's both done growed since I's been gone.

PHILIP (*merrily*).—And how thin you've got, Seline. You've lost flesh going to the country to your cousin's wedding.

SELINE.—My, my, jes' hear dat boy ! Do you think I'm slimmer, Mam'selle Dea? (*She looks at her fat sides.*) An' what's you chil'run been erdoin' all dis yere time dat I's been away? An' how's yer *pauv'* papa, Ma'mselle?

DEA (*sighing*).—He's very bad, Seline. He don't sleep.

SELINE.—My, my, honey, I's sorry ter hear sech bad newses. An' is yer done sole any yer little images while I's gone to der weddin'?

DEA.—No, Seline, not one. *Pauv'* papa's finished Quasimodo. I've got him in my basket. I'm to sell him for five dollars.

SELINE.—Well, honey, ef yer want ter sell him yer got ter stan' him out where people'll see him; 'taint no use ter keep him covered up in yer basket. I'm goin' ter give yer a corner of my table. (*She brushes some cakes and fruits aside and puts the image there.*)

DEA.—But the dust, Seline! Papa doesn't like them **to** get dusty.

SELINE.—Never mind der dust, chile; it'll blow off. It's der money we want, an' I don't see how yer goin' ter sell dat poor little crooked image. (*She looks at it contemptuously.*) But I'm goin' ter sell one of dem little images fer yer papa dis yere day, er my name ain't Seline. I ain't been right yere in dis place since en' durin' the war fer nothin'. I ain't made no fortune, but I's done made right smart, an' now I's got plenty to do a little fer you, honey, what ain't got no ma, only a *pauv'* sick papa, so I's going ter help yer sell yer little images. Yer tired an' sleepy, chile ; jest drap down on my little stool an' take a nap in der shade, an' I'll look out for customers. (*Dea goes to sleep behind the stand. Philip takes a position at the side and Seline comes round behind and waves a big fan over the fruit.*) Dar's dat stranger what useter pass yere right often fer flowers an' pralines. He's goin' ter buy yer little image if he comes ter day. He paints pictures up in der top of dat tall house down yere on Rue Royale, an' he's from der Norf, an' rich—rich. (*Dea sits up and looks pleased. They watch people pass them in silence.*)

MR. AINSWORTH *enters on the side nearest Philip, passes by him, then turns back and bends over tray of flowers.*

MR. AINSWORTH (*to himself*).—How fragrant! How delicious! (*He selects a bunch of flowers.*) Some pecans, please. (*He puts down a dime for the nuts. Both children watch him with wide-open eyes.*)

SELINE.—They're right fresh, M'sieur; an' won't yer have a few pralines for lagnappe?

MR. AINSWORTH.—Certainly; thank you. (*Looking at the children while Seline puts everything into a paper bag for him.*)

SELINE (*handing him the bag*).—If yer please, M'sieur, I'd like ter show yer dis yere little image. (*She shows him Quasimodo.*)

MR. AINSWORTH (*laying down flowers and bag, and taking up the figure very carefully*).—Who made this?

DEA.—My papa.

MR. AINSWORTH.—Your papa! Well, he's a genius. It is perfectly modeled. What's your papa's name, and where does he live? (*Dea drops her head and says nothing.*)

SELINE.—Her *pauv'* papa is al'ays sick. (*She touches her forehead significantly.*) He doesn't like to see no one. She would never tell strangers where she lives

MR. AINSWORTH.—Oh, I see. (*Gently to Dea.*) Well, my child, can you tell me what character this figure represents?

DEA.—It is Quasimodo.

MR. AINSWORTH.—Of course. It is perfect—perfect; but what a strange subject. (*He turns it over and over.*) Do you want to sell it?

DEA (*eagerly*).—Oh, yes, M'sieur. If you will buy it, *pauv'* papa will be so glad—he told me that I *must* sell it to-day.

MR. AINSWORTH.—How much do you ask for it?

DEA.—Papa said I could sell it for five dollars. Is five dollars too much? (*She hesitates.*) He said it was a work of art, but if you think it is too much—

MR. AINSWORTH.—It *is* a work of art. (*He draws out a five-dollar note from his pocket, but holds it.*) But tell me, if you can, how long it took your father to make this?

DEA.—Oh, a long time, M'sieur. I can't tell just how long, because he works at night when I'm asleep.

MR. AINSWORTH.—Ah! he works at night,—and do you sell many?

DEA.—No, M'sieur, I have not sold one for a long time.

PHILIP.—She hasn't sold one since Mardi Gras. A stranger bought one then, but he only gave three dollars for it.

MR. AINSWORTH (*smiling at Philip*).—Are you her brother?

PHILIP.—Oh, no, M'sieur, we are not related. She's just my friend. She's a girl, and I try to take care of her, and help her all I can.

MR. AINSWORTH (*to himself, as he turns away*).—How much he is like him,—the same look, the same smile, and about the same age. If Laura could see him, she would think her boy had come to life again. (*Turning back as if from a dream.*) What a good boy you are! She's a fortunate little girl to have such a friend. Tell me your name, please; I wish to get better acquainted with you.

PHILIP (*promptly*).—My name is Philip, M'sieur.

MR. AINSWORTH.—Philip! how strange! What is your other name?

PHILIP.—Oh, I'm always called Toinette's Philip. I never thought of any other name. I'll ask my mammy to-night if I've got another.

MR. AINSWORTH.—Is Toinette your mother?

PHILIP.—No, M'sieur, she's my mammy. She's a yellow woman, and you see I'm white.

MR. AINSWORTH.—Have you always lived with Toinette?

PHILIP.—Always, ever since I can remember.

MR. AINSWORTH.—Then you have no parents?

PHILIP.—Parents? Oh, no, I guess not. I don't know; I'll ask mammy.

MR. AINSWORTH.—Where do you live?

PHILIP.—I live on Ursulines street, away down town. Mammy has a garden and sells flowers. It's a right pretty garden. Won't you come some day to see it? Mammy's proud of her garden, and likes strangers to see it.

MR. AINSWORTH.—Thank you; certainly I will come. I like flowers myself, and I like pictures. I wonder if you like them—I mean pictures. I suppose you have not seen many.

PHILIP.—Lots of them, and I like them, too. I've seen them in the churches, and in the shop-windows—I've tried to make some.

MR. AINSWORTH.—Well, my boy, I'm a painter. I paint pictures. Would you like to come and see mine?

PHILIP.—Yes, M'sieur. I would if mammy says I may. I'll ask her, and if she'll let me, I'll come to-morrow.

MR. AINSWORTH.—I wish you could bring your little friend with you. I should like to paint a picture of her. (*Dea has been anxiously watching the note fluttering in his hand.*)

PHILIP.—Will you go with me, Dea?

DEA (*curtly*).—I can't—I must sell Esmeralda.

MR. AINSWORTH (*smiling from one to the other*).—So you have a figure of Esmeralda, and your name is Dea. Where is Homo, the wolf?

DEA.—Homo's under the table asleep, but he's not a wolf; he's only a wolf-dog.

MR. AINSWORTH (*to himself*).—Really, it is very interesting.—(*The dog comes forth.*) This child and the dog seem to have stepped out of one of Victor Hugo's books. (*He turns to Dea.*) My child, if you will come to my studio, I will pay you for your time, and I will buy some more of your little figures. I won't keep you long, and it will be better than staying in the street all day.

SELINE.—Yes, honey, so it will. Does yer understand? M'sieur'll pay yer, and yer'll have plenty money fer yer *pauv'* papa.

DEA (*hesitating*).—I'm afraid papa won't be willing. I'll ask him, but I must go home now. I must—I must go to papa.

PHILIP (*to Mr. Ainsworth*).—Dea can't promise now, but perhaps she'll come to-morrow. I'll try to bring her, M'sieur.

MR. AINSWORTH.—Thank you. I live in that tall house just below here. Ask the cobbler in the court to show you the way to Mr. Ainsworth's apartment. (*At last he hands the five-dollar note to Dea.*)

DEA (*with a look of gratitude*).—Oh, M'sieur, I'm so glad! Yes, I'll try to come; when *pauv'* papa knows how good you are, perhaps he'll let me come. And may I bring Esmeralda? Will you buy Esmeralda?

MR. AINSWORTH (*smiling*).—Yes, I'll buy Esmeralda. You'll find me a good customer, if you'll bring your figures to my studio.

DEA (*eagerly*).—I'll come—I'll come to-morrow! Now Seline, give me my basket. I must run all the way to papa.

SELINE (*soothingly, as she hands the basket*).—Don't, honey, don't get so flustered, an' don't run. It'll make yer little head ache, an' then yer can't get yer papa's dinner.

DEA.—I must—I must run, Seline. Au revoir, M'sieur. Au revoir, Philip. (*With a happy smile she runs out.*)

SELINE (*after watching Dea disappear*).—Oh, M'sieur, you've done a good deed buyin' dat little image. Pore child, she's so glad she can't wait, 'cause her papa ain't had no breakfast.

PHILIP.—Nor no supper last night. Dea don't like to tell, but I always know when they have nothing to eat.

MR. AINSWORTH (*in amazement*).—What! Is it possible? —nothing to eat! Are they as poor as that? And have they no one to take care of them?

PHILIP.—They haven't any one. They came here from France when Dea was a baby, and her father's been strange and sick ever since her mother died.

SELINE (*with a sigh*).—An' that poor chile has to take

care of him. Oh, M'sieur, do buy somethin' more fer the sake of that motherless little cretur !

MR. AINSWORTH.—I will—I certainly will. I'll try to do something for them. I'll sell some to my friends. Bring the child to me and I will see what I can do. Good day ! (*He goes out.*)

PHILIP.—Good day, M'sieur.

SELINE.—Good day, M'sieur. (*They watch him depart.*)

PHILIP.—I didn't think any one who painted pictures would stop to talk to us. Why, I ain't a bit afraid of him. You can bet I'm going to see him, and I'm going to get him to teach me to paint pictures.

SELINE.—An' he's rich !—He'll buy lots of them little images.

CURTAIN.

THE SICK BOY'S PLAN.

CHARACTERS.

Mr. Goodwin, *a clergyman.*

Mr. Crawson, *a fisherman, pale and hollow-eyed.*

Mr. Dodge, *a prosperous farmer.*

Jimmie Dodge, *a small boy just recovering from a serious illness.*

Mrs. Dodge, *his mother, a gentle woman.*

Servant.

Situation.—JIMMIE DODGE *was enticed by* DANIEL CRAWSON *to play truant. They quarreled over their pond-lilies and* DANIEL *struck* JIMMIE *on the head with an oar. He was taken home senseless. Finally* JIMMIE *gets better,* DANIEL *reforms and* JIMMIE *plans to surprise the kind doctor.*

The scene is in the ordinary living-room of a well furnished farm-house. Young people can take all the parts with proper costumes.

Enter REV. MR. GOODWIN *followed by* MR. CRAWSON.

MR. CRAWSON (*with great emotion*).—Now I'll tell the truth though it carries my own boy to prison for life. (*He blows his nose.*) My boy, Daniel, and he (*He points to the supposed sick room at one side.*) were in my boat. They had a quarrel about some lilies they had gathered. Daniel has a hot temper, and he struck Jimmy on the head with

88

his oar. If he's killed him, why——(*His emotions are too much for him. He goes out.*)

MR. DODGE *enters from the other side.*

MR. GOODWIN.—Have you seen Mr. Crawson? I never saw a man so changed. I am told he has not once left home or allowed his son to step over the threshold since the sad accident. He considers himself pledged to you not to let his son escape whatever the consequences may be.

MR. DODGE (*in a kindly tone*).—I remember nothing of that. I sincerely pity him.

SERVANT *enters.*

SERVANT (*to Mr. Dodge*).—Mr. Crawson, sir, has come back again and wants to see you, sir.

MR. DODGE.—Have him come right up here.

MR. GOODWIN.—Perhaps it would be better for me to retire. He may want to speak to you alone.

MR. DODGE.—That may be so. You can step right into that room, Mr. Goodwin. (*Mr. Goodwin goes out.*)

MR. CRAWSON *enters on other side.*

MR. CRAWSON.—I can't stand it any longer. I want to know what you intend to do to my son.

MR. DODGE.—I don't understand you, neighbor.

Mr. CRAWSON.—I mean in case of the worst. I know I ought not to come to you in your trouble; but I can't eat nor sleep till it's decided.

MR. DODGE.—Do you mean in regard to Daniel who struck the blow by which my son was injured?

MR. CRAWSON.—Yes.

MR. DODGE (*thoughtfully*).—Does he seem penitent?

MR. CRAWSON.—He's done little but cry ever since.

MR. DODGE (*heartily*).—Then tell him I freely forgive him, as I hope God will.

MR. CRAWSON (*staggering back*).—Do you mean to say that you sha'n't take him up,—commit him to jail for trial?

MR. DODGE.—I never thought of doing such a thing. Every day when I pray that God will give me back the life of my boy, I pray that this dreadful event may be blessed to his companion. You may tell him so. It would be in vain for us to ask God to forgive our sins, if we did not from the heart forgive each other. (*He shakes hands sympathetically with Mr. Crawson and goes out. Mr. Crawson sinks down in a chair and covers his face with his hands.*)

MR. GOODWIN *enters unobserved and puts his hands on* MR. CRAWSON'S *shoulders.*

MR. CRAWSON (*starting up and smiling*).—I believe it. I believe it. (*He seizes Mr. Goodwin's hand and shakes it.*) I always scoffed at religion. I allus said it did for Sunday use; but it wouldn't work for every day wear; but I believe it now; and Mr. Dodge has got it too. I must go home and tell my poor boy. (*He goes out.*)

MR. DODGE *returns.*

MR. GOODWIN.—I am very much pleased with what Mr. Crawson says and does.

MR. DODGE (*warmly*).—That man's heart is in the right place. Why, the doctor said——

MRS. DODGE *enters leading* JIMMIE *carefully forward.*

MR. GOODWIN (*stepping forward and putting his hand on the boy's head.*) How is Jimmie to-day?

JIMMIE.—I suppose I'm some better, but my head aches awfully yet.

MRS. DODGE.—There, dear, sit down here (*She leads him to one side where she sits in a chair and rolls up a cushioned stool for him beside her.*) and rest your head in mamma's lap. You can go to sleep if you want to.

MR. GOODWIN (*to Mr. Dodge*).—You were speaking of the doctor, Mr. Dodge.

MR. DODGE.—Yes, I was saying that Mr. Crawson, poor hard-working man that he is, went to the doctor and insisted on leaving a hundred dollars to pay for his attendance on Jimmie.

MR. GOODWIN.—I hope the doctor did not accept it.

MR. DODGE.—He did for the moment to ease Mr. Crawson's mind, but he afterward carried it back to the bank and put it to Mr. Crawson's credit again.

MR. GOODWIN.—That was right. The doctor too has his heart in the right place.

MR. DODGE.—You will think so when I tell you that he has just brought me his bill all receipted. I could not offend the good man by not accepting it; but I shall watch a chance to do him a favor.

MR. GOODWIN (*starting to go*).—Truly, the world has better people in it than we sometimes think. (*He goes out accompanied by Mr. Dodge.*)

MRS. DODGE (*looking at Jimmie, who stares up with wide-open eyes*).—Why, Jimmie, do you feel worse, darling?

JIMMIE.—No, mamma, but I've got a plan. I hope you and papa will be willing. (*She bends down and kisses him on the forehead.*) Do you think papa would sell his buggy? I heard him tell Mr. Morse it was too narrow for him, and that was the reason he bought the carryall. Now the buggy has been standing in the barn a long time, and he don't use it but once in a great while.

MRS. DODGE (*laughing and going to the door*).—Husband

come up here a minute.   Here is a boy wants to know if
you will sell your buggy.

MR. DODGE *enters, smiling.*

MR. DODGE.—Who wants it, Jimmie?

JIMMIE.—I do.   Oh, papa, please don't laugh.   I've been
thinking of a plan.   I don't want Mr. Crawson to take his
money out of the bank for me.   If I hadn't been a bad
disobedient boy, I shouldn't have gone in the boat, and
then Daniel couldn't have hurt me.   I don't want the doctor
not to have his pay because he isn't rich, and he goes to
see so many poor people who can't give anything.

MR. DODGE.—But what has that to do with my buggy,
my son?

JIMMIE.—I'll tell you pretty soon, papa.   You know the
money grandma gave me; and the bank book with my
name in it that's in your desk?

MR. DODGE.—Yes, I know.

JIMMIE.—Now, papa, if you'll take the money for yours,
and let me have the buggy, and get Mr. Morse to fix it up
and varnish it, then I could give it to the doctor instead of
his old, rattling thing.

MR. DODGE (*thoughtfully*).—That's a famous plan, Jimmie.
(*He rises and walks about room.*)   I thought you were
going to buy a watch and gold chain, and a Phi Beta Kappa
medal like the minister's, and a farm with your money in the
bank.

JIMMIE.—Oh, papa!   (*In shame.*)   That was when I
was a little boy.

MR. DODGE (*with a comical glance at his wife*).—Ah indeed, that makes a difference!   (*After a short pause.*)
Well, I can have the buggy-wheel mended, and the whole
painted to look as well as new for twenty dollars.   So if

you're inclined to make me a good offer, I think I shall take you up.

JIMMIE (*eagerly*).—Will the money I have be enough?

MR. DODGE.—Let me see. There's five hundred dollars besides the interest for four years and some little sums added. Yes, I think that will do.

JIMMIE.—Oh, papa, I'm so glad. (*He cries for joy and Mr. Dodge laughs heartily.*)

MRS. DODGE.—Hush! I wouldn't, husband. He only knows that he is very happy. Let us take him to his room now. He must not have too much excitement. (*She puts a shawl about him and Mr. Dodge carries him out.*)

MR. DODGE.—What will the doctor say? Do you think he'll know it is his? (*All go out.*)

A CHILD'S LOVE.

Sarah, *a small girl dressed to represent Spring.*

Hannah, *another small girl representing Summer.*

Samuel, *a small boy representing Autumn.*

David, *another small boy representing Winter.*

Situation.—*This dialogue is of a religious nature. The names are of Old Testament characters. There is little or no action in the dialogue, for it is meant for very little folks. There are four sets of speeches. The first set is about the Seasons ; the second set is about Animals ; the third set is about the Earth and Heavens ; the last set is about personal Friends. These different sets may be arranged in different ways, according to circumstances. A little group of four children may recite them all, or there may be four groups of children, or any set may be recited without the other sets.*

    The arrangement of the children on the platform will depend on the platform and the number of children used. If sixteen take part, they may form a perfect square—four in front. When these four have recited, they may file to the rear or to the side of the room, and so on to the end. If only four take part, each may step to the front to recite his stanza and remain standing there until the refrain has been repeated by all.

94

SARAH.— I love the spring, the gentle spring;
        I love its balmy air,—
        I love its showers, that ever bring
          To us the flow'rets fair.

ALL.— Come, let us sing, we love the spring,
        We love the summer too,—
        While autumn's fruit each one will suit,
          To winter give his due. '

HANNAH.—I love the summer's sky so bright;
        I love the fragrant flowers;
        I love the long, long days of light:
          But more the shady bowers.

ALL.— Come, let us sing, we love the spring,
        We love the summer too,—
        While autumn's fruit each one will suit,
          To winter give his due.

SAMUEL.— I love the autumn's clust'ring fruit,
        That in the orchard lies;
        I love its ever-changing suit,
          Its trees of brilliant dyes.

ALL.— Come, let us sing, we love the spring,
        We love the summer too,—
        While autumn's fruit each one will suit,
          To winter give his due.

DAVID.— I love stern winter's ice and snow;
        I love his blazing fire;—
        I love his winds that freshly blow,—
          Yes, winter I desire.

ALL.— Come, let us sing, we love the spring,
        We love the summer too,—
        While autumn's fruit each one will suit,
          To winter give his due.

SARAH.— I love the merry birds, that sing,
So sweet, their morning song,—
I love to see them on the wing
Speed gracefully along.

ALL.— Yes, we will love the gentle dove—
The birds that sing so sweet,
The fishes all, and insects small,
The beasts we daily meet.

HANNAH.—I love beneath the limpid wave
To see the fishes glide;
I love to watch them as they lave
So gayly in the tide.

ALL.— Yes, we will love the gentle dove,—
The birds that sing so sweet,
The fishes all, and insects small,
The beasts we daily meet.

SAMUEL.— I love each prancing, noble steed;
I love the dog, so true;
I love the gentle cow; indeed,
Without, what could we do?

ALL.— Yes, we will love the gentle dove,—
The birds that sing so sweet,
The fishes all, and insects small,
The beasts we daily meet.

DAVID.— I love the little busy bee;
I love the patient ant:
For they this lesson teach to me—
"We need not ever want."

ALL.— Yes, we will love the gentle dove,—
The birds that sing so sweet,
The fishes all, and insects small,
The beasts we daily meet.

SARAH.—   I love the blue and far-off sky;
           I love the beaming sun;
         The moon and stars, that, up on high,
           Shine bright when day is done.

ALL.—   We love, on high, to see the sky;
           We love the broad, blue sea;
         We love the earth, that gave us birth;
           We love the air, so free.

HANNAH.—I love the very air we breathe;
           I love, when flow'rets bloom,
         At early morn, or dewy eve,
           To inhale the sweet perfume.

ALL.—   We love, on high, to see the sky;
            We love the broad, blue sea;
         We love the earth, that gave us birth;
           We love the air, so free.

SAMUEL.—   I love the ocean, vast and grand;
           I love to hear its roar—
         I love its waves that kiss the sand,
           And those that proudly soar.

ALL.—   We love, on high, to see the sky;
           We love the broad, blue sea;
          We love the earth, that gave us birth;
           We love the air, so free.

DAVID.—   I love the broad and fruitful earth;
           I love each hill and dale;
         I love the spot that gave me birth—
           My own dear native vale!

ALL.—   We love, on high, to see the sky;
           We love the broad, blue sea;
          We love the earth, that gave us birth;
           We love the air, so free.

7

SARAH.—   I love my father, ever kind;
               I love to meet his smile,—
               I love to see him pleasure find
                 In watching me the while.

ALL.—   Our friends are dear, that we have here,
               But, better far than all,
               There's One we love, who dwells above,
                 And on His name we call.

HANNAH.—I love full well my mother dear;
               I love her cheering voice,—
               Her gentle words I wait to hear,–
               They make my heart rejoice!

ALL.—   Our friends are dear, that we have here,
               But better far than all,
               There's One we love, who dwells above,
                 And on His name we call.

SAMUEL.—   I love my little brother sweet;
               I love his words of glee,—
               I love his playful glance to meet,
                 His beaming smile to see.

ALL.—   Our friends are dear, that we have here,
               But better far than all,
               There's One we love, who dwells above,
                 And on His name we call.

DAVID.—   I love my little sister fair;
               I love her rosy cheek,—
               I love with her each joy to share,
                 Her happiness to seek.

ALL.—   Our friends are dear, that we have here,
               But better far than all,
               There's One we love, who dwells above,
                 And on His name we call.

(*They all bow and file out.*)

A MANLY BOY

CHARACTERS.

Mr. Jones, *a fleshy gentleman in a linen coat,—chairman of Committee on Church Decoration.*

Mr. Follins, *another gentleman.*

Dick Stuart, *a very manly little boy of about ten or twelve years.*

A Clerk.

Situation.—DICK STUART *comes to town on a very hot day in August to secure the job of furnishing evergreens for the church at Christmas. The men in the office laugh at evergreens at Christmas, but promise him the job. His honest, fearless face wins.*

The scene is in the business office of MR. JONES. *There is a desk, a desk chair and other chairs.* MR. FOLLINS *has a newspaper. The gentlemen should be dressed for very hot weather.* DICK *is neatly but very plainly dressed.*

MR. FOLLINS *enters with a newspaper and seats himself.* MR. JONES *follows, mopping his brow.*

MR. JONES (*seating himself by the desk*).—This is terrible, terrible!—Thermometer ninety-eight in the shade. I pity the horses——

CLERK *enters smiling.*

CLERK.—A boy to see you, Mr. Jones.

MR. JONES.—Ha! a boy is there? Well, ask him in.

99

Any body who ventures out in the street under such a sun ought to have important business. (*Both gentlemen look toward the door as the clerk goes out.*)

DICK *enters, taking a handkerchief from his pocket and wiping his brow.*

DICK.—I want to see Mr. Jones.

MR. FOLLINS (*waving his hand toward Mr. Jones*).—That is Mr. Jones.

DICK.—Are you the chairman of the committee to decorate St. Stevens' church?

MR. JONES (*pausing in astonishment*).—Hem! yes, I'm the one.

DICK.—Have you engaged your evergreens for Christmas, sir?

MR. JONES.—For Christmas? ha! ha! ha! we haven't begun to think of Christmas yet, my little fellow.

DICK (*in a matter-of-fact way*).—I want to get the job, if you please. I'll supply the evergreen as cheap as anybody. I know, it's a good while before Christmas; but mother says it's best to be in season when you're to do anything.

MR. JONES (*looks at Mr. Follins and laughs aloud*).—What is your name?

DICK.—Richard Monroe Stuart.

MR. JONES.—How old are you?

DICK.—Twelve last March.

MR. JONES.—Have you ever decorated a church before?

DICK.—No, sir; and I don't expect to decorate it this year. Mother says it takes tall men with ladders, to do that. I only want to supply the evergreens, I'll do it as cheap as any body, sir.

MR. JONES.—Where do you live, Richard?

DICK.—I live in Strawfield, sir. They always call me Dick at home. (*He smiles.*)

MR. JONES.—Is your father living, Dick?

DICK.—Oh, yes, sir. He is the minister in Strawfield.

MR. JONES.—And you are doing business on your own account?

DICK.—Yes, sir. One of our neighbors has a church to decorate every year; and he makes a good deal of money.

MR. JONES.—I suppose your parents are willing you should do this; I mean that they knew of your coming here?

DICK.—Mother does, sir, of course.

MR. JONES.—Why not your father, too?

DICK.—I want to surprise him. The people are poor; and so they can't give much salary. If I get the job, I'm going to buy a new buffalo robe. We've needed one for the sleigh a good while.

MR. JONES.—Whew! will it ever be cold enough to need buffaloes? (*Dick laughs.*)

MR. FOLLINS.—I don't know what Mr. Jones will do; but if I were the chairman of the committee, you should have the job. I approve of boys who tell their mothers everything.

DICK.—Thank you, sir. There's one thing I haven't told mother yet. Last spring our hod got broken. If I make enough I want to get her a new one.

MR. JONES.—Good, my boy. I guess you'll have enough besides for the buffalo robe. If you don't, it won't be a very profitable job. Shall you gather the evergreen yourself?

DICK.—Yes, sir, in the vacation at Thanksgiving. Mother says she thinks she shall have time to help me wind it evenings; and then, I can keep it fresh down cellar. Do you think, Mr. Jones, I can get the job?

MR. JONES.—Come here the first of November, and I will tell you. Our church is feeling rather poor this year; but if we decorate at all, you shall supply the evergreens. Here is my card. Shall you remember?

DICK.—Oh, yes, sir! I should remember you, and where you live, without any card; but I'll take it if you please.

MR. FOLLINS (*drawing out his portmonnaie*)—Suppose, Dick, that I give you enough to buy a hod now. It's inconvenient to do without one.

DICK (*with pride and some indignation*).—I'm much obliged to you, sir, but I'd rather earn the money for it. Mother'd like it a great deal better. (*Turning to Mr. Jones.*) I'll be sure to be back, sir, the first of November. (*He bows and starts out.*)

MR. JONES (*holding out his hand*).—Good-by, Dick. You've got a good mother, I'm sure.

DICK (*shaking the hand*).—Yes, sir. She's the best woman in the world. (*He holds out his hand to Mr. Follins who shakes it.*) Thank you, sir. (*He goes out.*)

MR. FOLLINS.—I'd give a hundred dollars if my boy had been here to see Dick. He'll make his mark in the world. He's got the true grit.

MR. JONES.—I'd give ten thousand if I had one like him. The idea of Christmas decorations on this hot day! Ha! Ha! Ha!

MR. FOLLINS.—I must go but I should like to be here the first of November. (*He shakes hands with Mr. Jones.*)

MR. JONES.—We shall hear of Mr. Richard Monroe Stuart again; or I'm mistaken. (*Mr. Jones follows Mr. Follins out.*)

A TINY QUARREL.

CHARACTERS.

Fanny, *a girl with a doll.*

Chrissie, *a girl who dislikes dolls.*

Situation.—CHRISSIE'S *father has given her a pony for Christmas. Her aunt has told her the story of a horse with wings, named Pegasus; so she has named him Wings. FANNY, her cousin, comes with her doll to visit her and wants to hear the story. The little girls quarrel and FANNY is on the point of departing when they make up and go off to give the canary a bath.*

> *A sofa is at the back of the platform and FANNY leaves her wraps on it. Near the front is a table with a work-basket on it, containing needles, thread, etc. There are chairs near by. The platform represents a sitting-room.*

> *Enter* FANNY *with her doll, and* CHRISSIE.

CHRISSIE.—Now, you must take your things right off and I'll find you a needle and thread.

FANNY (*taking off her cloak and hood*).—Well, then, I'll stay, 'cause there isn't much more to do to the cloak, and Queen Mab must have it right away.

CHRISSIE (*she has found a needle all threaded*).—There, won't that needle and thread do?

FANNY (*coming up to the table and taking the needle*).— Yes, I guess so. Now, while I'm sewing, you tell me that fountain story.

103

CHRISSIE.—Oh, yes! Only think. (*She settles down in a chair.*) It was a woman once, that fountain was; but - she poured her life all out into tears, crying because her son was killed. So the fountain is made of tears.

FANNY (*threading her needle*).—Bitter and salt, then.

CHRISSIE.—No, indeed; just as sweet and nice as any water. Pegasus loved it; and there was a beautiful young man, his name was Bel—Bel—well, I declare, I've forgotten,—no, 'twas Bellerophon; and he had a bridle, and wanted a horse. Oh, do you know this horse was white, with silvery wings, wild as a hawk; and once in a while, he would fold up his wings, and trot round on the mountain. (*Fanny yawns, and ties a knot in her thread.*) Oh, it was a splendid bridle, this man had, made of gold; and I forgot—the mountain the horse trotted round on was called Helicon. And the man mounted him, and went up, up, till they were nothing but specks in the sky.

FANNY.—A likely story! There, you've told enough! I don't want to hear any more such nonsense.

CHRISSIE.—Well, if you don't want to hear about the monster they killed, you needn't; that's all I can say; but the young man loved that horse; and he kissed him, too, he was so splendid.

FANNY (*looking very disgusted*).—Kiss a horse!

CHRISSIE.—Why, I've kissed my pony a great many times right between his eyes; and he almost kisses me. He wants to say, "I love you." I can see it in his eyes.

FANNY (*she has finished her doll's cloak and puts it on, and holds up the doll to be admired*).—I think her opera cloak is very bewitching, don't you, Chrissie? It's trimmed with ermine, because she is a queen, and is going to the opera.

CHRISSIE (*indifferently*).—It looks well enough, but it

isn't ermine. It's only white cat's fur, with black spots sewed on.

FANNY.—Of course it isn't real ermine, but I play that it is, and it's just as well.

CHRISSIE.—But you know all the while it's a make-believe. She hasn't any more sense than a stick of wood, either; and I don't see any sport in playing with dolls.

FANNY.—And I don't see any sense in fairy stories. Do you know what Harry says about you? He says your head is as full of airy notions as a dandelion top. I love Queen Mab as if she was my own sister. (*She is angry.*) You know I do, Chrissie. I always thought, if anything should happen to Queen Mab, and I lost her, I should certainly dress in mourning. Now, you needn't laugh.

CHRISSIE (*with a curl of her lips*).—Oh, I can't help laughing, when anybody makes such a fuss over a doll. Anything that isn't alive, and hasn't any sense, and don't care for you! I like canary birds, and babies, and ponies, and that's enough to like.

FANNY (*twitching at her doll's dress*).—Well, now, that's so funny, for the very reason I like my doll is because she *isn't* alive. I wouldn't have been you, Chrissie Redmond, when you had your last canary bird, and let him choke to death.

CHRISSIE.—Oh, no, Fanny, I didn't let him choke; I forgot to put any seed in the bottle and he stuck his head in so deep, that he smothered to death.

FANNY.—I don't know but smothering is as bad as choking, and now your new bird will be sure to come to some bad end.

CHRISSIE (*vexed*).—You're always saying hateful things. I like Jessie Thompson ten times as well, for she's a great deal more lady-like.

FANNY (*rising and going toward her wraps*).—Well, I suppose I can go home. You're such a perfect lady that I can't get along with you.

CHRISSIE (*to herself*).—Oh, dear, what does ail my tongue? (*Fanny puts on her cloak.*) Cousin Fanny, I wish you wouldn't go. I didn't mean to tell that I liked Jessie best; but it's the real honest truth, and if I should take it back, 'twould be a lie. (*Fanny puts on her hood and ties it with a twitch.*) But I like *you* ever so much, Fanny; now you know I do. You're hateful sometimes, but so am I; and I can't tell which is the hatefulest.

FANNY (*laughing merrily and throwing off her things*).— Yes, I'll stay just on purpose to plague you. (*She dances round the room.*)

CHRISSIE.—Oh, goody, what shall we do? Oh, I'll tell you. Just come out in the kitchen and see me wash my bird.

FANNY (*following with some surprise*).—Why, I thought birds washed themselves.

CHRISSIE.—They do, but Dicky won't. It's all in the world I have against Dicky. He isn't a cold-water bird.

(*They go out.*)

THE MOUSE.

Adapted from a story, " Toinette's Philip," by Mrs. C. V. Jamison.

CHARACTERS.

Madam Ainsworth, *an old lady, the head of a wealthy family in New York.*

Mr. Edward Ainsworth, *her son.*

Mrs. Laura Ainsworth, *wife to* EDWARD.

Philip Ainsworth, *a small boy, adopted son to* EDWARD *and* LAURA.

Lucille Van Norcom, *natural grand-daughter to* MADAM AINSWORTH *and heiress to the family estates.*

Mademoiselle, *a French governess to* LUCILLE, *of middle age.*

Helen, *a young maid to* LUCILLE.

Situation.—MR. *and* MRS. AINSWORTH *have seen* PHILIP *selling flowers in a street of New Orleans and have adopted him.* MADAM AINSWORTH *does not approve the choice and makes* PHILIP'S *life miserable, while she humors the fancies of* LUCILLE, *a delicate and whimsical girl, with grand manners.* PHILIP *resolves to get even with* LUCILLE. *He makes a cotton mouse and pulls it through the room where she is. She faints away. He is alarmed and confesses.* MADAM *threatens to take away his white mice, called by him* Père Josef's *" chickens" after the priest who gave them to him. He appeals so pathetically to her that she relents and he departs happy.*

107

The first scene takes place in a hall, the second in a sitting-room, the third in a study or library. Very little depends on the furniture used. A table and chairs of different kinds are used in all scenes. On the table in the first scene there is nothing; in the second scene there are books and magazines and a lady's work-basket; in the third scene there are letters and papers. These parts by proper dressing may all be taken by young people.

Scene I.

PHILIP *enters with a downcast air.*

PHILIP.—I don't see what I've done to hurt her. It's no use, she won't ever like me, and she treats me worse then she does the poodle, Fluff. (*He pulls out of his pocket a mouse made of wool with a long thread tied to it.*) I've got to get even with her, and she will be back in a little while. My, won't she be scared, but I've got to have some fun. (*He places the mouse on the floor, untangles his thread, and keeping hold of the thread retires through door on other side.*)

Enter LUCILLE, GOVERNESS *and* HELEN *the maid in street costume.*

GOVERNESS (*jumping up into a chair*).—Ah! Eh! (*She shrieks.*) Voila! (*She points at the mouse; all scream. Lucille climbs on a table.*)

MADAM (*without*).—What is it——what is the matter? Lucille, darling, are you hurt?

LUCILLE.—The mice, the white mice. They're in the hall, they're running all over the floor. Oh, oh, I am so afraid!

GOVERNESS (*hysterically, as she draws her skirts closer about her*).—Les souris, les petites souris, elles sont partout!

LUCILLE (*dancing with terror on the table*).—Where are

they? Oh, where are they? Are they running up the table legs?

GOVERNESS.—*Sont-elles sous la chaise ?*

HELEN (*she has been pursuing the mouse with her umbrella in vain*).—They're gone. They ran into the butler's pantry.

MADAM AINSWORTH *rushes in.*

MADAM.—Shut the door quickly before they get out. (*She hurries to Lucille and clasps the fainting child in her arms.*)—My dear, my darling ! oh, oh, you are faint.—Run and get my vinaigrette. Quick, quick ! fetch some water. The poor child is unconscious. (*She carries her to the sofa, and during a pause tries to revive her.*)

BASSETT *enters with solemn, impenetrable face.*

BASSETT.—'As hanything particular 'appened, Madam?

MADAM (*excitedly*).—Why, they went into your pantry, Bassett. (*She kneels by the sofa and rubs Lucille's hands.*)

BASSETT (*rubbing his hands in a puzzled way*).—What, Madam? What went into my pantry?

MADAM.—Why, the mice. Helen saw them run in there and *you* must have seen them.

BASSETT.—I didn't see nothing in my pantry, an' I've just come from there. If you'll allow me to say it, Madam, there's some mistake.

MADAM.—What ! do you mean to say that they didn't go in there—that boy's white mice, that he turned loose into the hall on purpose to frighten Miss Van Norcom?

BASSETT.—Bless me, no, Madam ! Master Philip's white mice never put a foot in my pantry.

HELEN (*with a twinkle of the eye*).—I saw them, or I'm sure I saw *one* ; perhaps it was the only one.

GOVERNESS.—I saw them running all over the floor.

LUCILLE (*she has recovered*).—Oh! I saw them climbing up the table legs.

BASSETT.—If you'll permit me, Madam, I'll venture to say that them little hinnocent hanimals of Master Philip's hain't never been out of their cage.

MADAM.—How dare you say such a thing, Bassett? Do you suppose that Miss Van Norcom and the others are mistaken?

BASSETT.—By no means, Madam. If I may be allowed to suggest, perhaps hit was what is called han hoptical hillusion.

MADAM.—Nonsense, Bassett! It was that troublesome boy's mischief. It is getting unendurable.

Bassett.—Will you hallow me to go to Master Philip's room, Madam? If the little hanimals are not there in their cage, I'll hadmit that they are 'id in my pantry. (*He marches out gravely.*)

MADAM.—What a shocking boy he is.—Lucille, I'm afraid you will be ill. You are so excited, so nervous. But don't fret, darling. (*To the Governess.*) He must be punished; he should not be allowed to distress Lucille in this way. We will help her to her room as soon as Bassett returns.

BASSETT *re-enters with a smile.*

BASSETT.—Hit's just as I hexpected, Madam. Them little hanimals are 'uddled hup together, sound asleep in their cage; and Master Philip is there 'ard at work a-studyin' of his Latin.

MADAM (*she gathers up Lucille, and Helen and the governess assist*).—It is certainly very strange, but I am not convinced. You can go to your pantry, Bassett. And when Miss Van Norcom is better I will investigate the matter. (*She goes out and all follow except Bassett.*)

BASSETT (*bowing low*).—Bless my 'eart, I've saved the

little pickle this time ; 'e 's safe if my young lady's young lady don't peach. She sees 'ow it is, an' she's too good to blow on the pretty little chap. I think 'e 's safe to get out of a bad scrape. (*He goes out on other side.*)

Scene II.

The curtain rises and shows PHILIP *reading a book and* MR. *and* MRS. AINSWORTH *talking as if in trouble.*

MRS. AINSWORTH.—It is absurd the way Lucille is encouraged in her silly fancies.

MR. AINSWORTH.—But it was not only Lucille, my dear. They all say they saw *something*. They could not all be mistaken. They could not all be the victims of " han hoptical hillusion," as Bassett says. Helen declares that *she* saw something, and Helen is not one to indulge in nerves.

MRS. AINSWORTH.—I don't know. I can't explain it. I only know Philip had nothing to do with it. I was in his room just before the outcry and the " children," as he calls them, were asleep in their cage, just as Bassett said. It is so unreasonable of your mother to suppose that Philip would let the mice out, and risk losing them, just to frighten Lucille.

PHILIP.—Mamma, may I go to my room? (*He rises and comes toward her.*)

MRS. AINSWORTH.—Certainly, my dear, if you wish to. You look pale. Aren't you well?

PHILIP.—I'm well, thank you, mamma; but—but I'm tired.

MRS. AINSWORTH.—Don't be unhappy, my dear, about this foolish affair. I'm sure we shall be able to convince Madam Ainsworth, when she is calmer, that *you* had nothing to do with it. (*He hesitates a moment, looks at her, kisses her warmly and goes out.*)

MR. AINSWORTH (*after a pause*).—Philip knows more about this than we think he does. I can tell by his manner that he has something on his mind.

MRS. AINSWORTH.—My dear, you are becoming strangely like your mother, with your absurd suspicions! How could the mice be asleep in their cage and running about the hall at the same time? I'm not surprised at your mother's unreasonableness. She dislikes the poor boy, and takes every means of showing it by her unkind accusations. But for *you* to suspect Philip! You who know how truthful he is!

MR. AINSWORTH (*cautiously*).—Did he *say* he knew nothing about it?

MRS. AINSWORTH.—I did not ask him. I would not hurt him so much as to have him think that I doubted his word. All he said was that the mice were not out of their cage; and I know he spoke the truth.

MR. AINSWORTH.—Well, Laura, we won't discuss it any more. But if I find that Philip is keeping anything back, I shall be greatly disappointed in him, for he's not the boy I thought he was.

MRS. AINSWORTH.—There is no reason why he should keep anything back. He is very brave, and not at all afraid to tell the truth. He is always willing to bear the consequences of his little pranks. He is never malicious—only mischievous—and where others would laugh at his harmless tricks, your mother treats them as if they were crimes. If *you* listen to your mother, she will succeed in turning *you* against the poor little fellow. Even now, I think you have changed toward him. He does not interest you as he did.

MR. AINSWORTH.—Now, my dear, *you* are unjust. I have not changed. I love Philip dearly, but I am not blind to his faults, and I do think he is a little—just a little—

malicious toward Lucille. Wouldn't it be better to speak to him gently and request him not to play any more practical jokes on that nervous, foolish child? Mother is so displeased, it will end in trouble between us if it goes on, and you must see how unpleasant that would be.

MRS. AINSWORTH (*rising and pacing to and fro*).—I am not disposed to make mountains out of mole-hills. The only thing for us to do is to take the boy away as soon as possible. We can never be happy here with him; your mother's dislike to him is unaccountable. (*She starts out.*)

MR. AINSWORTH.—Don't excite yourself, Laura. As soon as we hear that the priest is back we will start for New Orleans, and we may learn something from him about the boy that will relieve us of all responsibility. (*She goes out.*) Poor woman! She is changed! Why, the boy fascinated me the first time I saw him selling flowers in the street in New Orleans. Even after I had him dressed up and took him to our rooms, she was only half interested in him. And now she thinks I am changed toward him!—Well, well, we must go back to New Orleans and see if the old priest knows anything about his parents. The boy seems eager to return, too. To-morrow or next week at the farthest!— Ah! I have other matters to attend to! (*He goes out.*)

Scene III.

Private room of MADAM AINSWORTH. MADAM AINSWORTH
  *enters and sits at her desk opening letters. There is a
  knock on the door. She rises and opens it. In surprise, she steps back a little.*

PHILIP (*still outside*).—If you please, madam, may I come in? I want to tell you something.

MADAM (*coldly*).—Certainly, come in. I am very busy

this morning, but I will listen to what you have to say. (*She sits again at her desk and opens letters.*)

PHILIP *enters and stands near by.*

PHILIP.—I want to tell you about yesterday. It wouldn't be right not to tell you. I would have told last night, only for Mr. Butler. I don't want you to blame him. He wasn't to blame, he didn't know about it. I hid behind his pantry-door, when he was out. He didn't even help me make *it;* he never saw it. You won't blame him, will you? (*He looks imploringly at her.*)

MADAM (*sarcastically*).—Oh, Bassett was not an accomplice, then?

PHILIP.—He didn't know until after it was done. But he said he would stand by me. I don't mind for myself. You can punish me *good.* But poor Mr. Butler Bassett— I like him, and I don't want him punished.

MADAM.—Oh, I see, you are great friends. Well, go on with your interesting developments. I don't in the least understand what contemptible tricks you were up to.

PHILIP.—Why, you see, Lucille was so cross to me that I wanted—I wanted to pay her off. I wanted to frighten her. But I didn't want to make her ill. I wouldn't hurt her for the world. I wouldn't hurt any girl, even if she did—even if she did *curl her lip at me.* So I just thought it would be fun to make something like a mouse run across the floor.

MADAM (*triumphantly*).—Then there was something !

PHILIP.—Yes, there was. They did see something; but it wasn't one of the " children."

MADAM.—What was it?

PHILIP.—Why, it was a mouse, but not a live mouse. I made it out of wool, and put on a little tail of tape, and

the two eyes were jet beads off of Mademoiselle's fringe.
I tied a long black thread to it, and put it in the hall just
where Lucille would see it when she came in; and I made
it jump quickly by jerking the thread; and when I had
frightened them well, I pulled it into the pantry. Helen
tried to kill it with the umbrella; but she couldn't get a
lick at it. Then Lucille fainted, and Mr. Butler came in
and told me to run up the back stairs. So you see that
was why I said it wasn't one of the " children." (*He draws
a long breath.*)

MADAM (*angrily*).—Really, really! What—what decep-
tion!—what falsehood! And my son has boasted of the
boy's truthfulness!

PHILIP (*proudly*).—It wasn't a falsehood. I never tell
lies. It was only a—a mistake. It was because I went in
Mr. Butler's pantry, and I didn't want him blamed. That's
why I didn't tell at first. I'm very sorry now that I did
it. I'm very sorry that it made Lucille ill. And I came
to ask you to forgive me.

MADAM (*indignantly*).—Forgive you! Indeed, I shall
do nothing of the kind. I shall insist on your being punished
severely. You must be taught that you can't trifle in this
way with me.

PHILIP (*bravely*).—Well, I don't mind. You can punish
me. Only please don't blame Mr. Butler.

MADAM.—I shall settle with Bassett at my leisure. And
I shall order him to take those nasty little vermin out of
the house immediately.

PHILIP (*horrified*).—What vermin? You don't mean
Père Josef 's " children," do you ? They're not vermin.
They're just as good and quiet—and they're neat too ! I
keep their cage as clean as can be. Oh, you don't mean
that they must go?

MADAM (*with a cold, matter-of-fact tone and manner, she turns to her desk*).—I certainly do. I have had enough trouble since you brought the horrid little things here. I shall give the order to have them taken away at once. I don't care what becomes of them.

PHILIP (*advancing and laying his hand on her arm*).—Oh, Madam, *please* don't send them away. I can't let them go. Père Josef left them in my care. Oh, please, please, don't!

MADAM.—It is no use to make a fuss. I will not allow them to stay in my house; that is final. Now you may go. I am too busy to be troubled with such nonsense. (*She shakes off the little hand.*)

PHILIP (*overcome by sorrow, he clasps his hands and makes a pathetic appeal.*)—They're so little! They don't know any one but me. They'll be afraid of strangers. They may starve, they may get lost, and they can't find their way home, and what will Père Josef say when he sees me if I don't bring his "children" back? I promised to take care of them, and I can't if you send them away. I love them, so; they are so little and cunning and they love me. They're all I've got to care for. Don't send them away, please don't! (*She rises and looks at him.*) We're going home soon. Please let them stay with me till we go! Oh, please do, and I'll be so grateful. I'll try to be good; I won't tease Lucille again. I'll be so glad if you'll let them stay.

MADAM (*she turns away an instant to get control of herself*).—There, there, child!—that will do. Don't go on as if you were insane. If your heart is so set on those horrid little creatures, keep them, and oblige me by never speaking of them again. Now wipe your eyes and go to your room, and in the future try to treat Lucille properly.

PHILIP (*smiling rapturously*).—Oh, thank you, thank

you! I'll never forget how good you are, and you won't blame Mr. Butler, will you?

MADAM.—I'll consider it. He deserves to be reproved, but for your sake I may overlook his fault. (*He hurries out.*) It is certainly very strange. (*She has followed him with her eyes till he has gone.*) The boy quite unnerved me. I really felt for a moment as though he belonged to me. (*She goes out on other side.*)

NELL'S CHRISTMAS STOCKING.

CHARACTERS.

Nell, *a little girl, five or six years old, of happy trustful face.*

Huldah, *an older girl, of a thoughtful face.*

Louis, *a manly courageous boy, a little older than* HULDAH.

Cap, *the leader of a group of cowboys.*

Jim, Dick, *two other cowboys.*

Mrs. Jones, *a benevolent lady of middle age.*

Situation.—*The three children after the death of father and mother, have crossed the prairie in a covered wagon. They have now just stopped for the night on the outskirts of a town. It is Christmas Eve and all are thinking of the parents that are gone. The older children go to the village to buy presents for* NELL. *While they are away the cowboys ride up, take in the situation and depart. Later on, one of them fills the stockings to overflowing. The children are delighted the next day, and* MRS. JONES *invites them all to her home in the village where they afterwards live in comfort and happiness.*

The children should be dressed in worn clothes, but with some neatness. The cowboys should be in very négligé and picturesque costume, with a pistol and knife at the belt, and slouch hats.

The platform should look like an open prairie with the rear of the wagon just showing in the corner. There is needed only enough of the wagon to pin the stockings to and to form the flaps through which NELL pokes her head to speak to CAP. Of course there would be no chairs,—but only a stool or two. On one side is a fire with a kettle suspended over it on three sticks.

Scene I.

LOUIS, HULDAH *and* NELL *enter, apparently from the other side of the wagon.*

NELL.—Say, Louie.

LOUIS.—Well.

NELL.—Is to-morrow Christmas?

LOUIS.—Yes.

NELL (*she jumps up and down*).—Oh, goody! (*Louis and Huldah turn away in sorrow.*) We'll have another tree, won't we, Louie?

LOUIS.—I—I—I'm afraid not.

NELL.—Nor nothing in my stocking?

LOUIS (*feeling in his pockets and brightening up*).—Yes, yes, little one. You shall have *something* in your stocking, anyhow.

NELL.—Can't we have even a little teenty—tonty tree?

LOUIS.—I'll see, dear.

NELL.—Ain't there any old Mr. Santa Claus in this country?

LOUIS.—I guess so.

NELL.—'Vell, you must send him a letter soon as we get to that town, and tell him I want a tree, a *big* tree, with forty thousand bushels of things on it, and I shall go right to work now and pray real hard for what I want most. What shall I pray for for you, Louie?

LOUIS.—Oh, nothing.

NELL.—What, not even some merlasses candy?

LOUIS.—Oh yes, I'd like that.

NELL.—Well, I'll ask for that for you, and for a *lovely* blue silk dress and a perlanno to make music on for Huldah. (*Louis and Huldah advance apart to the front of the platform while Nell in the rear quietly takes off her stockings and pins them upon the outside of the wagon cover.*)

LOUIS (*to Huldah apart*).—We ain't got but forty cents in the world, Huldah, but I'd rather spend it all than have her get up in the morning and find them stockings empty.

HULDAH (*promptly*).—So would I. I couldn't bear to have her find nothing at all in them.

LOUIS.—I reckon she'd sleep sound enough and not waken if you and I went up into the town and bought her something for her stockings.

HULDAH.—Oh, yes; she never opens her eyes after she once gets to sleep, and there's no danger of her coming to harm here.

NELL (*she has just fastened her stockings up on the wagon cover*).—There now, it won't be the leastest bit of trouble for Santy Claus to stop here on his way to the town, and he can fill my stockings without even getting out of his sleigh. (*She climbs into the wagon.*)

HULDAH (*poking her head under the flaps of wagon cover*). —Now go to sleep, Nellie, as quick as you can and then Louis and I will see if we can find Santa Claus. (*To Louis.*) She is pretty tired and will drop to sleep very quickly. She will be asleep before we can get to town now. (*After a pause as they are gathering their cooking kettles.*) I wish we could have a home somewhere, Louis.

LOUIS.—We will, sometime. I want to get back east to the places I've heard mother and father talk about.

HULDAH.—Yes, you said that when we first started ever

so long ago but do you think the horse will pull us so far?

LOUIS.—I don't know, but pretty soon we will get to a town where I can find work and we'll stop there till spring. Perhaps you and Nell can go to school a few months.

HULDAH (*cheerfully*).—We'll get along some way, I reckon. Come, let's be off. (*They go out.*)

After some noise outside, enter cautiously three cowboys,
CAP, JIM, *and* DICK.

CAP.—That'd be a gay old rig to ride up an' down Fifth Avenoo in, wouldn't it?

JIM.—It's seen mighty tough times, that's sure. Wonder where the owner of such an elegant outfit is? If he ain't careful somebody 'll steal it. It ain't safe to let valuables lie round loose in this country for—well, I'll be everlastingly ding-fiddled—look there ! (*He points with his whip at the stockings.*) If some youngster ain't hung up its stockings for Christmas! (*Cap and Dick approach nearer.*)

CAP (*catching hold of the stockings*).—Well, old Santa Claus ain't filled it yet and I don't reckon—hello ! (*He starts back in surprise as Nell pushes her head through the flaps at the rear of the wagon.*)

NELL.—Are you Mister Santa Claus? (*All three men laugh.*)

DICK.—She caught you that time, Cap.

CAP (*to Nell*).—Well, who be *you* anyhow?

NELL.—I'm Helen May Hayden.

CAP.—Oh, you be, be you? Where's all your folks?

NELL.—I ain't got none, only just Louie and Huldah, and I s'pose they've gone off to hunt Santa Claus. Do you s'pose they'll find him?

CAP.—It's hard telling whether they will or not. What if they don't?

NELL (*puckering up face to cry*).—Then I s'pose my stockings 'll be empty in the morning, and they ain't never been empty a Christmas yet.

CAP.—Where 'd you come from, anyhow?

NELL (*thrusting out one arm*).—From the mountains way off yonder.

CAP.—And your dad didn't come with you?

NELL.—He couldn't—he's dead.

CAP.—Nor your marm?

NELL.—She's dead too.

CAP.—And there ain't nobody in the cart with you?

NELL.—No, ma'am—nobody.

CAP.—Who's Louie and Huldah?

NELL.—My brother and sister—and they're splendid. They'll find Santy Claus. Louie's got forty cents for him. I heard him tell Sis so.

CAP.—Oh, he has? Well I guess you'd better crawl back there and snuggle down among the bed-clothes till they come back. That's what you'd better do. Good night.

NELL.—Good night, mister. If you see Santy Claus you'll tell him 'bout my stockings? I wish you a Merry Christmas. (*She withdraws into the cart and they go off.*)

CAP.—Oh, yes. Good night, and sleep tight.

NELL.—Good night.

LOUIS *and* HULDAH *return quietly and put an orange in one stocking, and a toy lamb and a small bag of candy in the other.*

LOUIS.—I wish I could have got the big doll. How her eyes would have sparkled!

HULDAH.—And I know she'd 'most go crazy over that set of little dishes if she'd got 'em.

LOUIS.—Well, well, perhaps another time. (*They go out round the cart.*)

CAP *enters very stealthily with his arms full of bundles. He puts a fine doll, a purse of money and some dishes in the stockings, and ties some bundles to the cart.*

CAP (*after he has disposed of his bundles he stands off and looks at them an instant*).—Ah! if she hadn't died —and the child—its name was Nell too—a different fellow I'd have been. Perhaps I'd be settled down now in this very town, instead of scampering over the prairie like a wild cat. Well, it is not to be, an' I s'pose there's an end of it but— (*He goes off.*)

Scene II.

The next morning early, LOUIS *comes round the wagon.*

LOUIS (*in wild excitement*).—Huldah! Come here! come here quick! Look at that.

HULDAH *enters hastily.*

HULDAH.—Why the very doll! Who could have done it all? Where did they come from?

NELL *enters cheerily.*

NELL.—You did find Santa Claus, didn't you? I told him you'd find him.

LOUIS.—Told who?

NELL.—Oh, a real nice man. He came just after you'd gone. I thought he was Santy Claus and so I looked out and asked him and they all laughed.

HULDAH.—Who laughed, child? Were there more than one?

NELL.—Oh, yes, there were three of 'em; and one came up to the wagon and felt of the stockings and the others stood over there (*she points to where they stood.*) and kept laughing. I didn't like them.

HULDAH.—What did they say to you?

NELL.—They didn't say anything to me.   He talked to me.   He was real nice.

LOUIS.—Well, what did he say?

NELL.—He wanted to know where my father and my mother was and who you were—and I told him.

HULDAH.—And then?

NELL (*she has been untying the dishes*).—Oh! Oh! Oh! (*She dances with delight.*)   What pretty dishes!   Can't we all eat out of 'em to-day?   This is Christmas, you know.

HULDAH.—Yes, I guess so.

LOUIS.—But, Nell, did you tell us all the men did?

MRS. JONES *enters.*

HULDAH (*to Louis*).—Oh, here is the lady we saw at the church.   (*To Mrs. Jones.*)   Good morning, ma'am.

MRS. JONES.—Good morning, children.   Is this where you live?   (*She looks about her.*)   What a hard time you have had!

LOUIS.—Oh, not so awful bad, ma'am.   We've managed to get along.   If I could only get a job somewhere, we'd all stay and work.

MRS. JONES.—Well, now, this is Christmas and let's not worry about anything at all.   Would you all like to come to my home and eat your Christmas dinner?   Would this little girl?   (*She holds out her hand to Nell.*)

NELL.—Yes'm, if Louie and Huldah are going.   Can I take my doll?

MRS. JONES.—Certainly, of course.   Why, this is a very pretty new doll.

NELL.—Yes, Santa Claus brought it.

HULDAH.—Mrs. Jones, do we look respectable enough to go to your house to dinner?

MRS. JONES.—Oh, yes, indeed.

LOUIS.—Well, then we'll come. (*To Nell.*) Show Mrs. Jones your other presents, Nellie.

NELL.—Oh, yes, come this way, Mrs. Jones. (*She leads her out.*)

HULDAH.—She is a very kind lady, Louis, and perhaps she will help us get work.

LOUIS.—I think perhaps we are through with our journey in this old wagon. The poor old horse has done his work.

Huldah.—We'll miss him, won't we? But I hope we can all live together, whatever we do. (*They go out.*)

FATHER TIME'S GRANDDAUGHTERS.

CHARACTERS.

Old Year, *a maiden in torn and stained garments and worn-out shoes.*

New Year, *a younger maiden, in light, airy, fresh costume, with bright ribbons, etc.*

Father Time, *a youth, dressed as an old man, wrinkled and bent with age, with a long white beard.*

Watchman, *another youth, dressed in working clothes.*

Situation.—*A little before midnight,* OLD YEAR *gathers her possessions together to depart from the town. While she waits on the steps of the town or city hall, she is joined by* NEW YEAR, *her sister. With great affection they greet each other and converse together, until just as the bell strikes midnight* FATHER TIME *appears and ushers off* OLD YEAR *to join the sisters who have preceded her. Then* NEW YEAR, *too, departs about her own new duties.*

OLD YEAR carries in one hand a capacious bandbox, from which protrude all manner of things, and under her arm an immense folio, like the annual volume of a newspaper. NEW YEAR *carries only a small and pretty basket on her arm.* FATHER TIME *is dressed like a farmer and carries a sickle. The* WATCHMAN *has at*

126

his belt a bunch of keys and carries a lantern in his hand.

The dialogue takes place on the steps of the town hall, in the light of the full moon. Have the steps arranged at the side of the platform.

Enter OLD YEAR, *slowly and wearily. She approaches the steps and sinks down upon them. After resting a moment she places her bandbox carefully in full view at one side; then she draws the great folio out from under her arm and opens it upon her knees to look it over again.*

Enter NEW YEAR, *gayly.*

NEW YEAR (*after greeting Old Year cordially*).—Well, my dear sister, you look almost tired to death. What have you been about during your short stay here?

OLD YEAR (*disconsolately*).—Oh, I have it all recorded here in my Book of Chronicles. There is nothing that would amuse you; and you will soon get sufficient knowledge of such matters from your own personal experience. It is tiresome reading. (*She turns over the leaves of the folio.*)

NEW YEAR,—What have you been doing in the political way?

OLD YEAR.—Why, my course here in the United States though perhaps I ought to blush at the confession,—my political course has been full of changes, sometimes for the party in power and sometimes against it. Historians will hardly know what to make of me in this respect. But the Democrats——

NEW YEAR.—I do not like these partisan remarks. We shall part in better humor if we avoid all political discussion.

OLD YEAR (*with a sigh of relief*).—With all my heart. I have already been tormented half to death with squabbles of this kind. I care not if no whisper of these matters ever reaches my ears again. Yet they have occupied my attention so much of the time that I scarcely know what else to tell you.

NEW YEAR.—Have all the contentions been between political parties?

OLD YEAR.—No. In other ways blood has streamed in the name of Liberty and of Patriotism; but it must remain for some future, some far-distant Year to tell whether or no those holy names have been rightfully invoked.

NEW YEAR (*hopefully*).—Have energies been wasted, or have life and happiness really been thrown away?

OLD YEAR.—Well, who can tell? The ends often appear unwise and still oftener remain unaccomplished. But the wisest people and the best keep a steadfast faith in the upward and onward progress of mankind, and they hold that the toil and anguish of the path serve to wear away the imperfections of the Immortal Pilgrim, and will be felt no more when they have served their purpose.

NEW YEAR (*exultingly*).—Perhaps I shall see that happy day!

OLD YEAR (*smiling gravely*).—I doubt it. You will soon grow weary of looking for it and will turn for amusement (as I have often turned) to the affairs of some sober little city like this.

NEW YEAR (*caressing her*).—Why do you speak so?

OLD YEAR (*ironically*).—Oh, it would make you laugh to see how the game of politics is here played in miniature. The Capitol at Washington is the great chess-board, but even here burning Ambition finds its fuel; here (*exaggerated gesture.*) Patriotism speaks boldly in the people's behalf and virtuous Economy demands retrenchment in the emoluments of a lamplighter.

NEW YEAR.—Do you suppose I will talk like that in a year from now?

OLD YEAR.—Yes, yes. You may talk much worse. You will know more of human weakness and strength, passion and policy; for you can study them here almost as well as at the nation's centre. And there is this advantage that, be the lesson ever so disastrous, its tiny scope still makes the beholder smile.

NEW YEAR (*she puts her hand over her sister's mouth for an instant*).—Stop ! stop ! stop ! Tell me what you have done to improve the city? From what I have seen it looks old and worn.

OLD YEAR (*reflecting and turning over more pages of the big folio*).*—Ah, yes ! the street railways have been run by electricity for many a day, but the strangers that come here are more and more numerous because you see that they can depart more readily. There is a perceptible increase of oyster shops and other such establishments. But a more important change awaits this venerable town. An immense number of musty prejudices will be carried off by the free circulation of society. But (*She coughs.*) my breath is almost gone. (*She closes the big book.*) I must be going. (*She rises with the big book under her arm and seizes her bandbox.*)

NEW YEAR (*detaining her*).—Wait, sister, a moment more. Tell me what is in that great bandbox.

OLD YEAR (*she puts down book and opens bandbox*).—These are merely a few trifles which I have picked up in my rambles. I am going to deposit them in the receptacle of things past and forgotten. We sisterhood of Years never carry anything really valuable out of the world with us.

---

* Many local items may be inserted in this speech and in the other historical speeches of the Old Year.

Here (*She pulls out a bundle.*) are patterns of most of the fashions which I brought into vogue. You will supply their place with others. Here, put up in little china pots (*She produces a small pot.*) like rouge is a considerable lot of beautiful women's bloom; the disconsolate fair ones owe me a bitter grudge for stealing it.

NEW YEAR.—Of course they owe you a grudge.

OLD YEAR.—I have likewise a quantity of men's dark hair. I have left gray locks instead, or none at all. The tears of widows and others who have received comfort during the last twelve months are preserved (*She brings out an essence bottle.*) in some dozens of essence bottles, well corked and sealed. I have several bundles of love-letters, eloquently breathing an eternity of burning passion which grew cold almost before the ink was dry. Moreover here is an assortment of many thousand broken promises and other broken ware, all very light and packed into little space. The heaviest article is a large parcel of disappointed hopes; a little while ago they were buoyant enough to inflate a balloon.

NEW YEAR.—I have a fine lot of hopes here in my basket. They are a sweet-smelling flower—a kind of rose.

OLD YEAR (*discouragingly*).—They soon lose their perfume. What else have you brought to insure a welcome from these discontented mortals?

NEW YEAR (*with a smile of hesitation*).—Why, to tell the truth, little or nothing else, sister, except a few new Annuals and Almanacs, and some New Year's gifts for the children. But I heartily wish well to poor mortals, and mean to do all I can for their improvement and happiness.

OLD YEAR (*shaking her head*).—That is a good resolution, and by the way (*She turns to her bandbox.*) I have a plentiful assortment of good resolutions, which have grown so stale and musty that I am ashamed to carry them farther. Only for fear that the constable would arrest me, I should toss them into the street at once. There are many other things in my bandbox, but the whole lot would not fetch a simple bid, even at an auction of worn-out furniture; and as they are worth nothing either to you or anybody else, I will not trouble you with a longer list of them.

NEW YEAR.—And must I also pick up such worthless luggage in my travels?

OLD YEAR.—Most certainly, and consider yourself fortunate if you have no heavier load to bear. And now, my

Enter slowly FATHER TIME. *He remains in the rear for a moment.*

dear sister, I must bid you farewell.

TIME (*slowly and solemnly*).—Come, come, grand-daughter, your sisters are waiting for you to join them. There remains only a brief moment for me to offer your younger sister my customary advice as she enters on her new duties. (*He turns to New Year.*) Expect no gratitude nor good-will from this peevish, unreasonable, inconsiderate, ill-intending, and worse behaving generation. However warmly people may seem to welcome you, they will still be complaining, still craving what is not in your power to give, still looking forward to some other Year for the accomplishment of projects which ought never to have been formed, and which if successful would only provide new occasions of discontent. If these ridiculous people ever see anything tolerable in you, it will be after you are gone forever.

NEW YEAR.—But shall I not try to leave men wiser than I find them? I will offer them freely whatever good gifts Providence permits me to distribute, and will tell them to be thankful for what they have, and humbly hopeful for

more. And surely, if they are not absolute fools, they will
be happy, and will allow me to be a happy Year. For my
happiness must depend on them. (*She sits down on the
steps.*)

OLD YEAR (*sighing*).—Alas, for you, then, my poor sister!
(*She gathers up her burden.*) We, grandchildren of Time,
are born to trouble.

TIME.—Happiness, my children, dwells in the mansions
of Eternity. We can only lead mortals thither, step by
step, with reluctant murmurings, and ourselves must perish
on the threshold. (*The bell begins to strike the hour of
midnight.*) But hark! (*Turning to Old Year.*) Come
away with me. Thy task is done. (*They go out.*)

NEW YEAR (*she rises*).—Now, my task begins. Ah!
here comes the watchman.

Enter WATCHMAN *from opposite side.*

WATCHMAN (*looking at her curiously*).—A happy New
Year!

NEW YEAR.—Thank you kindly, sir! (*She picks a rose
from her basket and gives it to him.*) May this flower keep
a sweet smell, long after I have bidden you good-by! (*She
trips gayly out of the door through which Watchman entered.*)

WATCHMAN (*standing a moment and looking after her,
then putting the flower to his nose.*)—It smells sweet enough
now! (*He smells it again and goes out on the side opposite
to his entrance.*)

Handy Pieces to Speak.

Primary. 20 cts. ; Intermediate, 20 cts. ; Advanced, 20 cts.

ALL THREE FOR 50 CENTS.

Postage, 3 cts. each.

Model Card Selections for Recitation. Not Books but Cards.
A Separate Piece on a Separate Card for each Scholar.
A Sensible and Economical Arrangement.

These selections, just published on separate cards, supply a long felt want among teachers.   No waste material is included. Every piece has been carefully tested in the class room and found to be available. *If desired, they can be sold with profit by the teacher as low as two cents each card.*

For convenience in making use of these selections they have been classified as follows :

PRIMARY, 86 Selections.

INTERMEDIATE, 86 Selections.

ADVANCED, 86 Selections.

Each set, besides miscellaneous pieces, contains also several selections suitable for the Seasons, and the several Holidays.

This collection is made upon homœopathic principles.   The number of "Speakers" now published is enormous.   There are often a hundred selections in one book.   Yet the pupils usually find only about half a dozen available pieces in any of them.   It is believed that every selection in this series will be *used.*

The advantages of the card method of publication over the book form are apparent :

1. There is no padding.

2. The teacher can help a scholar to a "piece to speak" without a toilsome search through dreary volumes ; without the necessity of cutting long pieces down, or the risk of loaning valued books to careless fingers.

Each piece is printed on good, stout card board, and the cards belonging to each grade are enclosed in a heavy manila envelope with the contents printed on the cover.

Santa Claus and the Mouse, 12 v., 48 l. (for a boy or girl)——
The Christmas Gift, 5 v., 25 l. (for a girl) . . *Mary D. Brine.*
What Ted Found in His Stocking, 11 v., 42 l. (for a boy) —
Little Blue Eyes and His Christmas, 10 v., 40 l. (boy or girl) —
Patty's Dream, 32 lines (for a girl) . . . . *Clara G. Dolliver.*
O Dear ! 3 v., 18 l. (for a little boy) . . . . —— ——
The Dawn of New Year's Day, 6 v., 24 l. (for a little girl)–

Intermediate Grade.

Miscellaneous.

All the Children, 6 v., 48 l., ... —— ——
A Botanical Lesson, 13 v., 40 l. (young lady and six children)
The Twins of Italy, 13 v., 52 l. . . . . *Mrs. Wm. S. Carter.*
The Maiden and the Rainbow, 10 v., 40 l. (for a young lady)
Selling the Baby, 12 v., 48 l. (for a boy) . . . . *M. E. K.*
Hunting for Eggs, 9 v., 63 l. (for a boy or girl) —— ——
Indignant Nellie, 6 v., 58 l. (for a girl) . *Julia A. Mathews.*
A Fowl Proceeding, 6 v., 36 l. (for a boy) . . *H. A. Goodwin.*
The Coming Man, 6 v., 48 l. (for a young lady) —— ——
The True Story of Little Boy Blue, 17 v., 68 l. (young lady)
James' Methodism, 12 v., 48 l. (for a little boy) *A. T. Criss.*
Artie's " Amen," 8 v., 55 l. . . . . *Paul Hamilton Hayne.*

Seasons.

The First Fairy, 8 v., 32 l. (for a girl) . . . . . . *Susan Coolidge.*
A Bad Beginning, but A Good Ending, 4 v., 32 l. *M. Eytinge.*
The Three Culprits, 4 v., 24 l. (for a young girl) *M. D. Brine.*
Snowing, 6 v., 24 l. (for a young girl) . . . . . . *Susan Coolidge.*
Adelaide Goes to the Country, 60 lines (for a little girl) —
Vacation Song, 8 v., 32 l . . . . *Katharine Lee Bates.*
Baby's Rose-Leaf, 5 v., 20 l. (for a little girl) . . . . *E. L. B.*
The Children's Harvest Song, 5 v., 30 l. (for a child) ——
Jack Frost, 4 v., 32 l. (for a boy or girl) . . . . —— ——
A Crystal Wedding, 8 v., 64 l. (for a boy or girl) *J. Pollard.*
Outside and In, 3 v., 32 l. (for a girl) . . . . —— ——
Good-By Winter, 2 v., 20 l., (for a child) . . *Mary D. Brine.*

Holidays.

Jim's Fourth of July, 5 v., 46 l. (for a boy) . . *George Cooper*
Thanksgiving Turkey, 11 v., 44 l. (for a little boy or girl) —
How Robbie Shared Thanksgiving, 11 v., 44 l. (for a girl)—
Baby's Christmas, 5 v., 40 l. (for a young lady) —— ——
A Letter to Santa Claus, 7 v., 42 l. (for a girl) —— ——
Old Santa Claus, 9 v., 36 l. (for a little girl or boy)—— ——
Santa Claus, 4 v., 32 l. (for a young girl) . . . *John H. Yates.*
Sly Santa Claus, 5 v., 59 l . . . . *Mrs. S. C. Stone.*
Bessie's Christmas Party, 10 v., 60 l. (for a young girl) ——

The Jolly Young King, 3 v., 30 l. (for a boy) *M. D. Brine.*
Lily's New Year's Calls, 9 v., 54 l. (for a little girl) *G. Cooper.*
The Twelve Little Brothers, 4 v., 48 l.......*Helen G. Cone.*

Advanced Grade.

Miscellaneous.

What Ailed the Pudding? 9 v., 72 l. (for a young girl) ——
Auctioning Baby, 6 v., 48 l. (young lady and four children)——
The Little White Beggars, 6 v., 30 l. (for a young lady)——
Athirst, 10 v., 40 l. (for a young lady) *Mrs. M. Ella Cornell.*
Fairy Folk, 6 v., 36 l. (for a young lady and a little girl)——
The Coast-Guard, 5 v., 40 l. (for a boy) ..*Emily H. Miller.*
An Incident of the War, 83 lines (for a young man) ——
Mine Shildren, 6 v., 36 l. (for a boy)..*Chas. Follen Adams.*
Larrie O'Dee, 4 v., 40 l. (for a girl).........*W. W. Fink.*
An Open Letter to Henry Burgh, Esq., 7 v., 28 l. (young girl)
How a Paper is Made, 6 v., 48 l. (for a boy)... —— ——
The Owl Critic, 6 v., 77 l. (for a youth) ..*James T. Fields.*

Seasons.

The Year, 7 v., 28 l. (for a boy or girl)....... —— ——
What Makes a Bluebird? 7 v., 28 l. (little girl and young lady)
Apple-Blossoms, 7 v., 28 l. (for a young girl)........*H. H.*
Arbutus, 7 v., 28 l. (for a girl) ....*H. H.*
A Tell-Tale of Spring, 12 v., 48 l. (for a young girl)..*H. H.*
The Little Quakeress, 13 v., 52 l. (for a girl) ..
A Summer Day, 4 v., 24 l. (for a young lady).. —— ——
The Foot of the Rainbow, 5 v., 49 l. (for a young lady)——
An Autumn Question, 8 v., 32 l. (for a young girl)—— ——
Bidding the Sun "Good-night" in Lapland, 10 v., 40 l. (for
    a boy or girl)..............................*J. Allison.*
Thankful, 5 v., 40 l. (for a young lady)....... —— ——
The Way of the World, 6 v., 36 l. (for a young lady) ——

Holidays.

Grandma's Story, 6 v., 44 l. (for a youth).... —— ——
A Wild-Goose Chase, 16 v., 64 l. (for a young lady) ——
Where do you Live? 7 v., 56 l. (for a boy) *Josephine Pollard.*
A Winter Song, 4 v., 24 l...........*Susan Hartley Swett.*
A Christmas Carol, 6 v., 48 l. (for a boy or girl) *A. A. Proctor.*
Christmas Eve, 6 v., 48 l. (for a young man)... —— ——
McFlarity's Christmas Gift, 10 v., 60 l. (for a youth) ——
Christmas, 5 v., 30 l. (for a girl or boy).....*Susan Coolidge.*
After Christmas, 26 lines (for a young girl).... —— ——
What Santa was about Last Week, 102 lines (for a young lady)
New Year's Day, 4 v., 32 l. (for a girl)....... —— ——
New Year's Calls, 27 v., 81 l.................*Lizzie Burt.*

Pieces for Every Occasion

By Caroline B. LeRow

Compiler of "A Well-Planned Course in Reading"

Bound in cloth　　　　　　　　　　　　　　　　**Price, $1.25**

The selections included in this volume are in harmony with the spirit of class room work, which demand brevity, simplicity, good sense and sound morality. This is the only compilation of the kind in which these matters are considered as of equal importance with elocutionary effect. *Very few of the pieces are to be found in any other book.* That Miss LeRow has provided pieces for every occasion, the following summary bears evidence. The volume contains

Pieces for Lincoln's Birthday
Pieces for Flag Day
Pieces for Washington's Birthday
Pieces for Easter
Pieces for Arbor Day
Pieces for Decoration Day
Pieces for Graduating and Closing Days
Pieces for Fourth of July
Pieces for Thanksgiving Day
Pieces for Christmas
Pieces for New Years
Concert Recitations
Selections for Musical Accompaniment
Pieces for Other Less Observed Occasions

The observance of our poets' birthdays has become such a pleasant and profitable custom in our schools, that pieces have been provided for these anniversaries as well. *Besides these selections for special occasions, there will be found a large number of recitations suitable for almost any occasion.*

You may be interested to know that we also publish Handy Pieces to Speak, price 50c., Acme Declamation Book 50c., Three-Minute Declamations for College Men $1.00, Three-Minute Readings for College Girls $1.00, Pieces for Prize Speaking Contests $1.25, New Dialogues and Plays (*primary, intermediate* and *advanced*) $1.50, Commencement Parts (*valedictories, salutatories, essays,* etc.) $1.50, Pros and Cons (*both sides of live questions fully discussed*) $1.50—any of which we shall be glad to send you *on approval.*

HINDS, NOBLE & ELDREDGE, Publishers

31-33-35 West 15th Street　　　　—　　　　New York City

Pieces for Every Occasion

By Caroline B. LeRow

Compiler of " A Well-Planned Course in Reading "

Bound in cloth   Price, $1.25

Miscellaneous.

Miscellaneous—*Continued.*

Selections for Musical Accompaniment—
Continued.

Poets' Birthdays.

WILLIAM CULLEN BRYANT.

RALPH WALDO EMERSON.

OLIVER WENDELL HOLMES.

Poets' Birthdays—*Continued*.

Temperance.

The Seasons.

Flowers.

Lincoln's Birthday.

Lincoln's Birthday—*Continued.*

Decoration Day—*Continued.*

TITLE			AUTHOR
Flowers for the Fallen Heroes,	.	.	*E. W. Chapman,*
For Our Dead,	. . .	.	*Clinton Scollard,*
Little Nan,	. .	.	. . .
Memorial Day,	. .	.	*Margaret Sidney,*
Ode for Decoration Day,	. .	.	*Henry Peterson,* .
O Martyrs Numberless, .	.	.	. .
Our Comrades,	. .	.	. . .
Our Heroes' Graves,	. .	.	. .
Our Honored Heroes, .	.	.	*S. F. Smith,* .
Sleep, Comrades, Sleep,	. .	.	*H. W. Longfellow,*
The Heroes' Day, ..	. .	.	. .
The Silent Grand Army,	. .	.	*E. M. H. C.,*
The Soldier's Burial,	. .	.	*Caroline Norton,*

Flag Day.

No Slave Beneath the Flag, .	.	.	*George Lansing Taylor,*
Ode to the American Flag,	.	.	*Joseph Rodman Drake,*
Our Cherished Flag,	. .	.	*Montgomery,*
Our Flag,	. . .	.	*Henry Ward Beecher,*
" Rally Round the Flag! "	.	.	*A. L. Stone,*
The American Flag,	. .	.	*Henry Ward Beecher,*
The Flag, .	. .	.	*Henry Lynden Flash,*
The Flag of Our Country,	. .	.	*Robert C. Winthrop,*
The Flower of Liberty, .	. .	.	*Oliver Wendell Holmes,*
The Stars and Stripes, .	. .	.	. .

July Fourth.

A New National Hymn,	. .	.	*F. Marion Crawford,*
" Fourth of July," .	. .	.	*J. Pierpont,*
Freedom's Natal Day, .	. .	.	*Elizabeth M. Griswold,*
The Declaration of Independence,	.		*John Quincy Adams,*
The Nation's Birthday, .	. .	.	*Mary E. Vandyne,*
The New Liberty Bell, .	. .	.	*H. B. C.,* . .
The Principles of the Revolution,	.		*Josiah Quincy,* .

Labor Day.

Idleness a Crime,	. . .	.	*Henry B. Carrington,*
Knights of Labor, .	. .	.	*T. V. Powderly,*
Labor, .	. . .	.	*Rev. Orville Dewey,*
No Excellence without Labor,	.	.	*William Wirt,*
Opportunity to Labor, .	. .	.	*Thomas Brackett Reed,*
The Dignity of Labor, .	. .	.	. . .
Toil, .	. . .	.	. .
Work, .	. . .	.	*Thomas Carlyle,*

Thanksgiving.

Christmas.

New Year's.

CPSIA information can be obtained at www.ICGtesting.com
Printed in the USA
LVOW09*0110240216

476364LV00013BB/225/P